Table of Contents

Introduction

Types of Stories

- contemporary fiction
- fables
- science fiction
- tall tales
- historical fiction
- poetry
- folktales

Ways to Use the Stories

1. Directed lessons
   - with small groups of students reading at the same level
   - with an individual student

2. Partner reading

3. With cooperative learning groups

4. Independent practice
   - at school
   - at home

Things to Consider

1. Determine your purpose for selecting a story—instructional device, partner reading, group work, or independent reading. Each purpose calls for a different degree of story difficulty.

2. A single story may be used for more than one purpose. You might first use the story as an instructional tool, have partners read the story a second time for greater fluency, and then use the story at a later time for independent reading.

3. When presenting a story to a group or an individual for the first time, review any vocabulary that will be difficult to decode or understand. Many students will benefit from a review of the vocabulary page and the questions before they read the story.

Types of Skill Pages

Four pages of activities covering a wide variety of reading skills follow each story:

- comprehension
- vocabulary
- organizing information
- structural analysis
- parts of speech
- literature analysis and creative writing

Ways to Use the Skill Pages

1. Individualize skill practice for each student with tasks that are appropriate for his or her needs.

2. As directed minilessons, the skill pages may be used in several ways:
   - Make a transparency for students to follow as you work through the lesson.
   - Write the activity on the board and call on students to fill in the answers.
   - Reproduce the page for everyone to use as you direct the lesson.

3. When using the skill pages for independent practice, make sure that the skills have been introduced to the reader. Review the directions and check for understanding. Review the completed lesson with the student to determine if further practice is needed.

Stormalong

An American Tall Tale

Stormalong was a big baby. He outgrew his cradle a week after he was born. By the time Stormalong celebrated his first birthday, he had to sleep and eat in the barn with the horses because the house was too small. Before Stormalong blew out the candles on his second birthday cake, he was taller than the church steeple. When Stormalong was five years old, his mother knitted a hammock that stretched from New Bedford, Massachusetts, to Newport, Rhode Island. His father tied one end of the hammock to a giant pine tree in New Bedford and sailed down the coast to Newport. Then he fastened the other end to the top of an enormous chestnut tree.

"There, now," said his mother. "It will take you a few years to outgrow this bed."

Stormalong loved the sea and the ships. From his hammock bed, stretched between Massachusetts and Rhode Island, he could watch ships come and go. He knew when the fishing ships sailed into port and what they brought home. "The *Barstow* is on her way in with a load of halibut and cod," he shouted when he saw the *Barstow* heading for land.

When the people in town heard Stormalong's announcement, they rushed to the dock to buy fresh fish and welcome the crew home.

Stormalong knew all the ship captains. He signed up as cabin boy on the biggest ship he could find, the *Goliath*. All went well as long as he stayed in the middle of the ship. If he leaned over the port side of the ship, the crew had to run to the starboard side so the ship wouldn't roll into the sea. Stormalong could scrub the decks, throw out the anchor, or turn the wheel faster than the rest of the crew.

By the time Stormalong was eleven, he had outgrown the *Goliath*. He decided to build the biggest ship that ever sailed the ocean. It would take many tons of lumber to construct a ship that large. Stormalong didn't want to cut down all the trees near New Bedford. He liked the birds singing him to sleep each night when he slept in his hammock. He knew they needed trees in which to build their nests. He solved the problem by chopping down three trees from each forest from the Atlantic Coast to Pennsylvania.

To earn money for food and tools, Stormalong carried basket loads of fish from ships anchored in the bay to the towns along the shore. The water was never higher than his knees. He talked to ship captains and learned all he could about the oceans and ships.

By the time Stormalong finished building his ship, he was thirteen. He'd taught himself everything there was to know about reading, math, and the stars. He didn't need a crew. He could do everything a hundred seamen could do and do it much faster at that. He signed on a crew of five cooks and four cats. The latter were to keep the rats from boarding the ship and the former were hired to prepare meals for Stormalong and the cats. He christened his ship *Colossus*.

When the ship was loaded with food and the sails were in place, Stormalong swam across the harbor and pulled the ship into deep ocean water. He climbed up the ship's ladder and set sail. The *Colossus* was as fast as it was large. In no time at all it had reached the tip of South America. The *Colossus* didn't quite make the turn when it tried to squeeze between South America and Antarctica. It rammed into South America and broke the tip into small islands and pieces of land. After that there was a passageway called a strait through South America. Smaller ships could sail between the islands and get from one side of South America to the other. It was a good shortcut.

Stormalong sailed on to China, India, and many islands along the way. He traded for exquisite silks and finely decorated china dishes. He took on bags of pepper and tea leaves. In two months time he was back in New Bedford. He sold everything on the ship and became a very rich man. He tried to settle down on land, but he couldn't stay. It was too crowded. Everywhere he went he had to be careful he didn't step on a house or garden.

With his crew of cats and cooks, Stormalong sailed to the Caribbean Sea. Just as he was passing Florida, a tremendous hurricane tore at the sails of the *Colossus*. Ships sailing nearby were being tossed to and fro and swamped with water. Stormalong jumped overboard and swam through the towering waves. He piled as many boats as he could on the deck of the *Colossus*. He pulled sailors from the water and put them safely in the hold of his ship. The storm raged on.

Stormalong put the anchor chain between his teeth and swam toward Florida, pulling the ship against the wind and torrential rains. He pushed the ship up onto the beach, where waves dashed against it for two days and nights. When the storm finally wound down, the sailors climbed down the ladder of the *Colossus* to thank Stormalong.

After everyone had left the ship, Stormalong went back on board. He unfurled the sails to see if they could be repaired. A great wind, the last breath of the hurricane, hit the sails. The sails flapped like the wings of a giant albatross, lifting the ship and Stormalong into the sky. Stormalong waved good-bye and sailed off. If you look at the night sky, just as sailors often do, you might see the light from Stormalong's lantern flashing across the sky. That's the *Colossus* and Stormalong sailing across the immense ocean of air that surrounds the earth. It's the only sea big enough for a giant sailor and the largest ship that was ever built.

Questions about *Stormalong*

1. Stormalong's mother made him a special place to sleep. Describe it.

   _____

   _____

2. Why did Stormalong decide to build his own boat? What was unique about the boat?

   _____

   _____

   _____

3. What did Stormalong name his boat? Why do you think he chose that name?

   _____

   _____

4. What happened when the *Colossus* tried to go around the tip of South America?

   _____

   _____

5. Some people say Stormalong had a big heart. Why?

   _____

   _____

6. In your own words, tell about Stormalong's Caribbean adventure. Use the back of the paper if you need more space.

   _____

   _____

   _____

Name _____

Stormalong

Vocabulary

Match each word from the story with its definition. Use the clues in the story to help you decide what each word means.

steeple	hammock	port	starboard	halibut
anchored	latter	former	christened	strait

1. _____, _____ right and left sides of a ship

2. _____ a bed of woven cord, strung between two places

3. _____ a tower on a church

4. _____ a large edible fish; a flounder

5. _____ a narrow passageway of water

6. _____ the second one mentioned

7. _____ named a ship

8. _____ the first one mentioned

9. _____ held in place by a heavy object attached to a chain

- -

Fill in the blanks in the sentences using the best answer from this list of words.

tremendous	immense	raged	exquisite	unfurled

1. Stormalong _____ the sails to see if they could be repaired.

2. The storm _____ for two days causing _____ damage and flooding.

3. There is an _____ ocean of air surrounding the earth.

4. The _____ jewels in the crown sparkled under the bright lights.

Name _____

Stormalong

Synonyms

A **synonym** is a word that means the same or almost the same as another word.

Write the number of each word on the line in front of its synonym.

List 1   **List 2**
1. christened   _____ saw
2. rushed   _____ first
3. immense   _____ tied
4. watched   _____ hired
5. fastened   _____ enormous
6. signed on   _____ welcomed
7. latter   _____ hurried
8. former   _____ last
9. greeted   _____ named

Choose a word from List 1 above to complete each sentence below.

1. Everyone in town _____ to the dock to buy fresh fish and

_____ the crew.

2. He _____ his ship the *Colossus*.

3. The _____ ocean of air was the only place big enough for a
   giant sailor.

4. He _____ ships come and go from his hammock bed.

5. He _____ five cooks and four cats.

6. He _____ the other end to the top of an enormous
   chestnut tree.

7. The _____ were to keep the rats from boarding the ship, and

   the _____ were hired to prepare meals for Stormalong.

Name _____

Stormalong

Exaggeration

Exaggeration is an important part of the type of stories called tall tales. The heroes and heroines of the tales are gigantic and extravagant. The exaggerated feats of courage and endurance gave early settlers encouragement to face the task of developing a new land.

Find examples of exaggeration in *Stormalong* that support each of the statements below. Write the examples on the lines following each statement.

Stormalong was a big baby.

_____

_____

_____

Stormalong earned money to build his ship.

_____

_____

_____

Stormalong didn't need a crew.

_____

_____

_____

Stormalong rescued ships and sailors from a Caribbean hurricane.

_____

_____

_____

Iggie

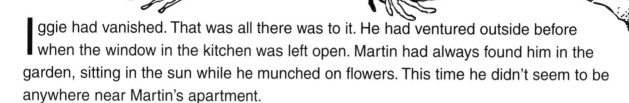

Iggie had vanished. That was all there was to it. He had ventured outside before when the window in the kitchen was left open. Martin had always found him in the garden, sitting in the sun while he munched on flowers. This time he didn't seem to be anywhere near Martin's apartment.

A year ago someone had left an iguana in a box at the pet store where Aunt Belle worked. She guessed that the iguana was too big for his owners to take care of, or they didn't want him anymore. The store didn't have a cage big enough for a full-grown iguana, so Aunt Belle brought him home. That was just a week before Martin's birthday. Iggie was the best present Martin had ever received.

Now Martin was worried. It was getting colder at night, and iguanas needed to stay warm. He and his friend Arnold searched the garden, looking under all the bushes. They knocked on apartment doors and talked to the people who were home. Mr. Kennon had seen an iguana outside the laundry room early that morning.

Martin and Arnold searched the laundry room. They looked behind the machines, under the tables, and even inside the washers and dryers.

"Maybe he got locked in someone's apartment by mistake," Arnold said. "We could check it out. He likes to sit in the windows."

Martin and Arnold walked around the apartments. The lady who lived in the apartment above Martin's jerked her blinds shut when she saw them looking in her window. In the next apartment, Aunt Mary (everyone called her that even though she wasn't anyone's aunt) just waved and said, "Come on in."

Martin and Arnold asked Aunt Mary if she had seen Iggie.

"I've been in and out all day. I had to do some laundry for Sis since she's been sick," said Aunt Mary. "I drove a big basket of clothes over to her apartment, but I didn't see that iguana of yours. If I had seen that green, scaly creature, I would have hollered real loud. You know I'm not much for animals without fur. I hope you find him real soon, and I hope I don't."

Martin and Arnold searched under the cars and all around the parking lot. "Iggie would like the warm pavement here, but this sure wouldn't be a good place for an iguana," said Martin. A car zoomed into a parking space.

"Right!" said Arnold. "He'd be so scared that he'd lose his tail here for sure." They didn't find any long tail lying around on the pavement.

"Let's look through the garbage cans," said Martin. "He might smell something he wants to eat there. There are always bugs around too."

They borrowed some gloves from Angela, the maintenance person. Holding their noses with one hand and shaking the garbage cans around with the other, Martin and Arnold looked in all the cans. There weren't any long tails or spiny backs poking out of the garbage.

Martin set a bowl of mealworms and a piece of banana outside his apartment door. "He won't eat unless he's warm," worried Martin, "but I guess it won't hurt to leave something out for him." As the sun went down, Arnold went home for dinner. Martin sat on a tall stool by the kitchen window while he ate his potato soup. Every few minutes he looked around outside.

"You might as well give up for now," Aunt Belle said. "Iggie probably found himself a warm spot for the night." Martin thought Aunt Belle looked worried. She kept looking out the windows too.

A warm spot! She was right, Martin thought. Iguanas always headed for the warmest place around. But he'd looked everywhere warm he could think of—the parking lot, the dryers in the laundry room. Then Martin remembered what Aunt Mary had said about taking the laundry to her sister's apartment. Hot laundry right out of the dryer was a perfect place for an iguana.

"Aunt Belle," Martin called. "I've got to talk to Aunt Mary right away."

"Her number's by the phone," Aunt Belle answered.

It didn't take long to convince Aunt Mary that they ought to take a look at her sister's basket of laundry.

Aunt Mary talked to Aunt Belle on the telephone before she stopped by for Martin. Then she drove Martin across town to Sis's apartment. "Don't get your hopes up, Martin. I'm sure I would have noticed Iggie's long tail poking out of the laundry basket if he crawled in there."

Aunt Mary knocked on Sis's door and called out, "It's me again. I brought company." Sis unlocked the door.

Sis was sitting up in a chair watching TV. "Funny joke," she said to Aunt Mary. She pointed to a motionless Iggie stretched out on top of the TV. "Where did you get such a real-looking stuffed toy? I think it's real cute on top of the TV."

Martin and Aunt Mary laughed. Iggie climbed down the front of the TV and made his way toward Martin.

Aunt Mary's sister shrieked, "It's got batteries!"

Martin set Iggie on his shoulders. "It's really Martin's pet iguana, not a toy," said Aunt Mary. "He must have crawled into the laundry basket this morning and hidden under the warm clothes."

"I can't believe I let a live lizard sit on my bed," Sis said. "I carried it around the house this afternoon and showed it to my neighbor."

"Next time you're sick, I'll bring Martin and Iggie for a visit," said Aunt Mary. "You look a lot better now. *Iguana sitting* seems to agree with you."

Name _____

Questions about *Iggie*

1. Aunt Belle gave two reasons why she thought people had left Iggie at the pet store. What were they?

   _____

   _____

   _____

2. List the places Martin and Arnold looked for Iggie.

   a. _____

   b. _____

   c. _____

   d. _____

   e. _____

3. What gave Martin the idea that Iggie might have hidden in Aunt Mary's sister's basket of clothes?

   _____

   _____

   _____

4. How was it possible that Sis thought that Iggie was a stuffed toy?

   _____

   _____

   _____

5. What kind of a person do you think Aunt Mary is? Use clues in the story to explain your answer.

   _____

   _____

   _____

Name _____

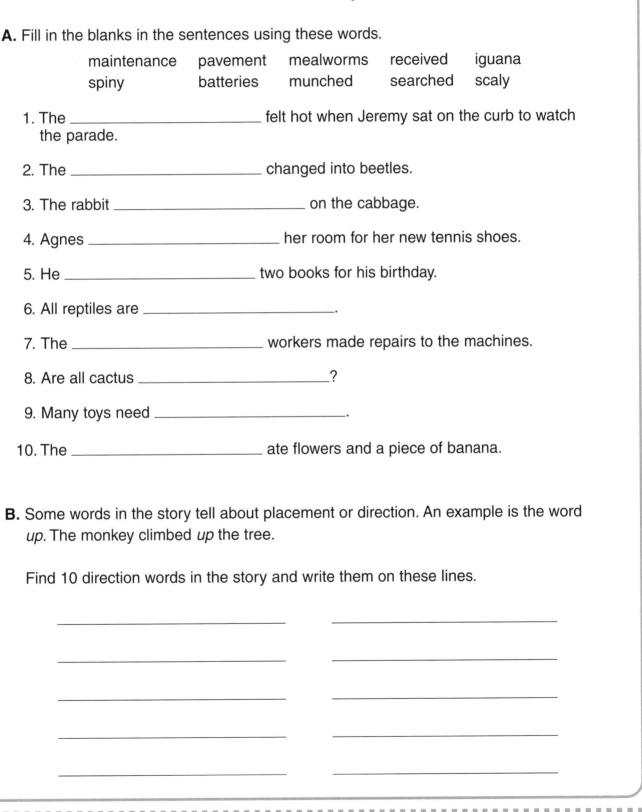

Iggie
Vocabulary

A. Fill in the blanks in the sentences using these words.

maintenance   pavement   mealworms   received   iguana
spiny   batteries   munched   searched   scaly

1. The _____ felt hot when Jeremy sat on the curb to watch the parade.

2. The _____ changed into beetles.

3. The rabbit _____ on the cabbage.

4. Agnes _____ her room for her new tennis shoes.

5. He _____ two books for his birthday.

6. All reptiles are _____.

7. The _____ workers made repairs to the machines.

8. Are all cactus _____?

9. Many toys need _____.

10. The _____ ate flowers and a piece of banana.

B. Some words in the story tell about placement or direction. An example is the word *up*. The monkey climbed *up* the tree.

Find 10 direction words in the story and write them on these lines.

_____   _____

_____   _____

_____   _____

_____   _____

_____   _____

Name _____

Iggie
Compound Words

Compound words are two words that are joined together to make another word. For example, a *coatrack* is a rack for coats. A *backyard* is a yard in back of a house.

1. Three of the compound words in the story are *someone*, *without*, and *afternoon*. Write a sentence about the story using each of those compound words.

   _____

   _____

2. Find three other compound words in the story. Write them on these lines.

   _____   _____

   _____

3. Combine each word from the first column with a word from the second column to make a compound word. Write your compound words on the lines.

   blue   dated   _____

   house   foot   _____

   fire   time   _____

   side   car   _____

   street   sticks   _____

   bare   bird   _____

   bread   walk   _____

   out   boat   _____

   over   wood   _____

   some   due   _____

Name _____

Iggie
Action Verbs Crossword Puzzle

The following verbs, or forms of the verbs, are found in the story. Use the clues and write the words in the crossword puzzle.

Word Box					
wave	holler	convince	knock	sneak	crawl
looks	search	guess	zoom	walk	shriek

Across

1. sees
3. to move on hands and knees
4. to suppose or estimate
6. to look for
9. to rap on a door
10. to motion good-bye or hello with the hand
12. to yell loudly

Down

2. to scream
5. to try to get by something without being seen or caught
7. to make someone believe something
8. to move quickly
11. to move on foot at a regular pace

The Boy Who Didn't Know Fear

An Adaptation of a European Folktale

In the kingdom of Near and Far, there lived a boy who didn't know fear.

One morning his mother said, "I want to pick fresh blackberries for a pie, but I fear the great bear that lives in the forest."

"What is fear?" asked the boy.

"Fear is when you feel worried that something terrible will happen to you," answered the mother.

"I can't imagine how that would be," said the boy. "I must find fear and see for myself. I'll go to the berry patch." The boy took a pail for the berries and an ax to cut wood for a fire. Off he went.

He came to a sleeping giant. The boy looked into the giant's pockets. "No fear here," he said. Then he peered into the giant's ears. "Nothing terrible there." The boy walked into the giant's nose. "Hello," he called, "I'm looking for fear." His voice echoed in the giant's nose.

"Aaah-choo!" the giant sneezed. The boy flew out of the giant's nose and landed on top of a tall pine tree.

"I'm allergic to people. They make me sneeze!" bellowed the giant.

"Your sneeze blew me up into the tree," said the boy. "I'm looking for fear."

"Fear, is it?" the giant roared. "I'll show you fear." The giant pulled the boy's tree out of the ground and sent it sailing through the air.

"I'm flying over the forest like a bird!" shouted the boy. "I can see farms and villages. There's no fear in the sky."

When the tree came down, it splashed into the sea. It rolled over and over, but the boy held on. When the tree stopped spinning, the boy said, "I didn't find any fear in the air or under the water."

The boy chopped off two limbs of the tree with his ax. He paddled his tree toward shore. It started to rain. Lightning streaked down from the sky. The winds blew his tree onto the land. The boy found a cave and crawled inside. "Now I'm inside the earth. I'll try to find fear under the ground." The boy felt around the cave. He found a warm, furry bed.

When the boy stretched out on the bed, there was a tremendous roar. The bed rolled over.

"It must be the great bear," said the boy. "Now I'll find fear." The boy shook the great bear's legs. "Wake up," he said. The bear shuddered and went back to sleep. The boy shouted in the bear's ear and poked her with a tree limb. The bear bounded out of the cave. The boy followed her, waving the tree limb. "Wait!" yelled the boy. The bear ran faster.

"Mother was wrong," said the boy. "I felt no fear when I saw the bear." The boy filled his pail with blackberries and walked back to his village.

There was a crowd of people in the town square. "Can you help me find fear?" the boy asked a farmer.

"I'm too busy," said a farmer. "Every hundred years a new judge is chosen to settle arguments. Today the old judge will throw a laurel wreath over the crowd. If it lands on my head, I'll be the new judge."

The boy crossed the square. He heard cheers and felt the laurel wreath fall on his head. The crowd carried him to a towering throne. There he would sit for the next one hundred years. He would listen to people's arguments and try to make everyone happy. For the first time, the boy felt fear.

Questions about
The Boy Who Didn't Know Fear

1. Why didn't the mother want to pick blackberries?

   _____

   _____

2. Why was the boy looking for fear?

   _____

   _____

   _____

3. What dangers did the boy find that did not make him feel fear?

   a. _____

   b. _____

   c. _____

   d. _____

4. When the boy was judge, what would he have to do?

   _____

   _____

5. Why did the boy feel fear when he became the village judge?

   _____

   _____

   _____

Name _____

The Boy Who Didn't Know Fear

Antonyms

Antonyms are words that have opposite meanings. Examples of antonyms are *tall–short* and *quiet–loud*.

A. Find the antonyms for the following words in the story. Write the antonyms on the lines.

1. emptied _____

2. right _____

3. cold _____

4. night _____

5. stale _____

B. There are many pairs of antonyms in this story. One example is the name of the place where the boy lived, the village of *Near* and *Far*. Find each word below in the story and circle it. Then find the antonym for each word in the story. Circle the antonym and write it on the line.

1. went _____

2. here _____

3. sky _____

4. under _____

5. ran _____

6. started _____

7. new _____

8. in _____

Name _____

The Boy Who Didn't Know Fear

Vocabulary

1. Fear is an **emotion**, or feeling, that you have when you are in danger. **Envy**, **happiness**, and **anger** are other emotions. Which of these three emotions would you feel if each of these things happened to you?

   a. _____ Your brother or sister ate your piece of chocolate cake.

   b. _____ Your friends have new bicycles.

   c. _____ You finished your homework early so you can watch your favorite TV program.

2. Write about a time when you felt each of these emotions.

   a. fear: _____

   _____

   b. envy: _____

   _____

   c. happiness: _____

   _____

   d. anger: _____

   _____

3. Use the clues in the story to match these words with their definition.

   towering   laurel wreath   peered   tremendous   allergic

   a. _____ dark green leaves tied in a circle

   b. _____ huge, enormous

   c. _____ very tall

   d. _____ what you are when something makes you sneeze or itch

   e. _____ looked into something

The Boy Who Didn't Know Fear

Setting

The **setting** of a story is where and when it takes place.

Answer these questions about the setting of *The Boy Who Didn't Know Fear*.

1. Where does the story take place?

   _____

   _____

2. List several different locations in the kingdom.

   _____

   _____

   _____

3. At what time of year do you think this story might have taken place?

   _____

4. What clue or clues helped you to choose the time of the story?

   _____

   _____

The Day Pecos Bill Rode Old Twister

An American Tall Tale

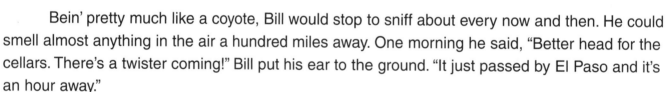

You've probably heard about Pecos Bill, the Texas wrangler who was as tall as a two-story house and as strong as an ox. When it was time to round up the cattle and drive them to Abilene, Bill just pointed his nose toward the sky and let out a coyote howl that echoed across Texas. The cattle thought there were a hundred or so coyotes coming after them. They were so spooked, they stampeded in the other direction as fast as they could. Pecos Bill had cowpunchers stationed all along the trail. They kept the cattle running in the right direction. When the cattle slowed down, Bill just let loose with another howl. The cattle kept running until they all reached Abilene in record time.

You might think it was strange that Bill could howl like that. Bill, you see, came by it naturally because coyotes raised him. Some folks say he thought he was a coyote until he was fourteen years old. Seems he got lost from his folks when they were moving west. But that's a story for another day.

Bein' pretty much like a coyote, Bill would stop to sniff about every now and then. He could smell almost anything in the air a hundred miles away. One morning he said, "Better head for the cellars. There's a twister coming!" Bill put his ear to the ground. "It just passed by El Paso and it's an hour away."

That was enough time to get some of the cattle into the tunnel Bill had dug out using Rattler, his pet snake, as a drill. As soon as everything was in order, the cowhands headed for the cellars.

"You coming in?" yelled Cowpoke Carl.

"I'm gonna ride this one out!" shouted Bill.

Carl shut the wood cover to the cellar and bolted it in place.

As for the rest of the story, this here's how Bill told it when he showed up a week or two later. There isn't any doubt it was the truth. Bill was as truthful as a Sunday school teacher.

It seems Bill and his horse, Bulldozer, waited until Old Twister came roaring across the ranch like an angry panther chasing its dinner. When it caught sight of Bill, it took out after him.

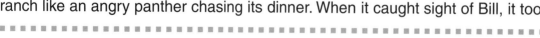

Bill led Old Twister away from the barns and the bunkhouse as far as he could. Bulldozer managed to dance to the side each time Twister came close to Bill. That big wind was racing at such a speed, it could only twirl straight ahead like a ballerina spinning across the stage. It couldn't keep up with Bulldozer's fancy stepping. Old Twister was getting uglier by the minute. It wasn't used to playing a losing game of tag. It was clear to Bill that Old Twister wouldn't slow down until it tore up the whole ranch and him too.

"I've tamed bears, snakes, and wolves," Bill said to Bulldozer. "I guess it's time I took the fight out of a twister. My rope's ready, and I'm going for the ride of my life. Bulldozer, you head out as far away from me and this bag-of-wind as you can. Leave the rest to me."

Bill sent his rope whirling into the air faster than a bolt of lightning. It dropped over the top of Old Twister and headed for the middle of that windy monster. Bill tightened the rope and gripped the end. Hanging on like a flea on a dog, he jumped onto the side of the twister and climbed toward the top. Old Twister danced, hopped, and nearly turned itself wrong side out trying to shake Bill off. It was some fight, but Bill never did give up. He just climbed higher, poking his spurs right into Old Twister's sides.

When Bill reached the top, he was a little worse for wear. His hair stood straight up like the points on a picket fence, and his leather shirt was so fringed it looked like blades of brown prairie grass. Nonetheless, he was as calm as a hibernating bear. He rode bareback on the rim of that twister, and looked down inside. There was a city's worth of houses, a herd of cattle or two, and everything else you could need just swirling around inside. Old Twister bucked and kicked up its tail like a bucking bronco at a rodeo. It didn't do any good. Bill rode Old Twister like he was a kid riding on a rocking horse.

Now Bill was having so much fun, he decided there ought to be some good done along the way. It was a shame to let Old Twister smash up all those houses. People moving west had a long stretch to travel without a town. Bill reached down inside, and one by one he tossed the houses behind Old Twister. The houses settled down in neat rows, making up the prettiest town you could imagine. Now, when people crossed that long, dry stretch of prairie, they'd have a place to stop and rest.

Bill scooped up all the grass and plants inside the twister and threw them into a giant stack near the town. He dug in his spurs each time the twister tried to roar off across the prairie. While the twister spun around in circles going nowhere, Bill was scooping out the cattle and dropping them onto the stack of grass. They'd have enough to eat until the next wagon train came rumbling along. When Bill finished, it looked like a fine place to settle down. One day, Bill planned to do just that.

Old Twister was empty now and as tired as a mother hen that had spent the day chasing after her chicks. Bill led Old Twister back the way it came. By the time Bill was back at the ranch, Old Twister was a little breeze as gentle as a newborn lamb frolicking across a meadow. Bill had had enough traveling for a while. He went back to howling at the moon and riding Bulldozer around the ranch.

Name _____

Questions about
The Day Pecos Bill Rode Old Twister

1. Describe the way Pecos Bill drove the cattle to Abilene.

    _____

    _____

2. How did Pecos Bill learn to howl like a coyote?

    _____

    _____

3. How did Pecos Bill know there was a twister coming?

    _____

4. How did Pecos Bill catch the twister?

    _____

    _____

5. Why did Pecos Bill think that Old Twister wouldn't stop until the ranch was torn down?

    _____

    _____

6. What did Pecos Bill do with the cattle and the houses caught up in the twister?

    _____

    _____

7. What happened to the twister?

    _____

    _____

The Day Pecos Bill Rode Old Twister
Vocabulary

A. Write the words below next to their meanings. Use the clues in the story to help you decide what the words mean.

twister	stretch	bareback	fringe	stationed	bunkhouse
spooked	stampeded	cellar	ballerina	gripped	

1. _____ a place where cowboys sleep

2. _____ a long distance

3. _____ frightened

4. _____ held on tight

5. _____ positioned at a certain place

6. _____ an underground room

7. _____ a tornado

8. _____ a dancer

9. _____ riding without a saddle

10. _____ loosely hanging strips

11. _____ ran wildly

B. There are four words in the story that mean "people who herd or work with cattle." Write the words on these lines.

1. _____   3. _____

2. _____   4. _____

The Day Pecos Bill Rode Old Twister

Similes

A **simile** is a comparison of two different things. It can describe a person or an action. Similes use the words *as* or *like*. For example: *Pecos Bill is as tall as a barn.*
The bear roared like a rocket blasting off.

There are many similes in the story. Find a simile in the story that tells about each of these sentences.

1. Pecos Bill was truthful.

   _____

2. Pecos Bill was tall.

   _____

3. His hair was straight up.

   _____

4. His shirt was shredded.

   _____

5. He was calm.

   _____

6. The twister bucked and kicked.

   _____

7. The twister was tired.

   _____

8. The twister was a gentle breeze.

   _____

9. Old Twister came roaring across the ranch.

   _____

The Day Pecos Bill Rode Old Twister

Exaggeration

Tall tales are stories that are exaggerated and couldn't really happen. The reader knows that the author is not serious because the story is ridiculous.

Here are two exaggerations from the story about Pecos Bill and the Twister:

Pecos Bill let out a howl that echoed across Texas.

Bill rode Old Twister like he was a kid riding on a rocking horse.

List eight more exaggerations from the story.

_____

_____

_____

_____

_____

_____

_____

_____

_____

_____

_____

_____

_____

Belling the Cat

An Adapted Fable

"Something must be done," said Percy. He collapsed on the floor of his mouse house. He sobbed and his body shook uncontrollably.

"You poor dear," said his wife, Agatha. She pulled him across the floor to their nest and covered him with a blanket. "It's the cat again, isn't it?"

"Indeed it is," said Percy. "He had his claws in my tail. I escaped by biting his paw. It's the third time this week that that fanged monster has caught me. I shudder to think what will happen to me, good wife. How will you and the children manage if I am eaten by the cat?"

"Don't even mention it!" replied Agatha. "You must not take any more chances."

"Then how will we eat?" asked Percy. "The cat hides in the kitchen. He hears every paw-step no matter how quiet. Three of our friends were taken by that fiendish feline last week."

"It's very unfair. There is so much food wasted here. Surely the people in this house could share. Perhaps we could ask the farmer's wife to deliver it to our door. Then we wouldn't have to bother with the cat or the kitchen."

"Good wife, you don't understand at all. The people who moved into our house with the cat are selfish and they despise mice. There are traps everywhere. I know how to stay away from the traps, but the cat is a sneaky, cruel creature. He has hiding places, and pounces on anything that moves. Hard-working, honest mice like ourselves will never be safe as long as that cat prowls the house."

"Well then, I suppose we must move," said Agatha. "There must be a house, a barn, or a store where we are welcome. After all, we do clean the floor of all crumbs and scraps. We are quite useful, I believe."

"Even if we knew of a safe place we could call home," said Percy, "we would never get past the cat and out the door with our nest and our children."

"For the life of me, I can't think of any way," said Agatha.

"It will be dangerous, but I will call a meeting," said Percy. "We can travel inside the walls and meet in the bedroom closet without running into the cat. We will discuss this problem sensibly and surely find the answer."

The next morning Percy tapped a mouse SOS on the wall. Every mouse from the attic to the basement scurried between the walls to the big closet in the farmer's bedroom.

Percy clapped his paws for silence. "We are all aware," he began, "of the dangerous creature that lurks in every corner of this house waiting to devour us. If we stay in the walls, we will starve. We must find a way to stop that cat."

Before Percy said another word, there was a horrifying yowl and scratching at the closet door. Sharp claws reached under the door, just missing Percy as he jumped away.

"Tomorrow in the attic," Percy squeaked. One by one the mice squeezed through the crack in the closet wall and hurried to their homes. Percy was the last to leave. He scrambled through the crack just as the closet door swung open and the snarling cat rushed at the tiny opening.

Percy heard the farmer's wife say, "Wonderful, clever Mr. Cat. Were you trying to catch those terrible mice that roam the house? You've caught three this week. In a month's time you will do away with all the mice just like you did in our last house, won't you?" Percy peered through the crack. The farmer's wife was petting the cat, which purred and snuggled in her arms.

"Disgusting," said Percy to his wife. "How could anyone be fond of a cat?"

The next morning all the mice climbed the inner passageway to the attic. When all the mice were quiet, Percy began again. "I have called everyone here to find a solution to our problem. If we leave our homes, who knows what other dangers we will find. We would have to flee for our lives, leaving all our possessions. Who has the answer?"

All the mice squeaked stories about their encounters with the cat. Finally, Leah, one of the newest mouse residents, stood by Percy and raised her paw for silence.

"The problem is very simple," said Leah. "If we knew where the cat was, we could stay away from him. When I lived in a barn, the barn cat had a bell on her collar. We always heard her coming and hid where she couldn't reach us. All we have to do is place a bell on the cat's collar."

"Why didn't I think of that?" said Percy. "A belled cat would be dangerous, but not as dangerous. All in favor of placing a bell on the cat's collar, squeak yes."

Every mouse except Agatha squeaked. She held up her paw. "Very clever indeed!" she said. "Now which one of you brave mice will volunteer to place the bell on the cat's collar?"

Every mouse was quiet.

Name _____

Questions about *Belling the Cat*

1. How had life recently changed for the mice?

   _____

   _____

2. What two ideas did Agatha suggest to avoid being eaten by the cat?

   _____

   _____

   _____

3. Why did Percy think her ideas wouldn't work?

   _____

   _____

4. Why did the mice have to meet a second time?

   _____

   _____

5. What did Leah think the mice should do about the cat?

   _____

   _____

6. At the end of the story, why didn't any of the mice answer Agatha's question?

   _____

7. What do you think the mice should do?

   _____

   _____

Name _____

Belling the Cat
Vocabulary

A. Use context clues in the story to determine the meaning of each word in the list below. Then write each word on the line in front of its definition.

uncontrollably   doze   replied   selfish   despise   feline   cruel   fond
sensibly   inner   solution   possessions   encounters   volunteer   devour

1. _____ to offer to help without receiving pay for the work

2. _____ to eat up hungrily

3. _____ meetings

4. _____ items belonging to someone

5. _____ unable to stop or acting in a way that can't be stopped

6. _____ to hate

7. _____ an answer to a problem

8. _____ in a way that shows good judgment

9. _____ mean, causing others pain

10. _____ answered

11. _____ inside; interior

12. _____ thinking only about oneself

13. _____ like, love

14. _____ belonging to the cat family

15. _____ to sleep

B. Write sentences using each of these words:

despise   encounter   sensibly

_____

_____

_____

Name _____

Belling the Cat
Point of View

In the story, the mice, the cat, and the people have different ideas about each other. Each has a different **point of view**.

1. What words in the story describe the cat from the mice's point of view? Look for the missing words and write them on the lines.

   a. _____ monster

   b. _____ feline

   c. sneaky, _____ creature

   d. _____ paw

   e. _____ yowl

   f. as long as that cat _____ the house

   g. _____ creature that _____ in every corner

   h. "_____," said Percy to his wife. "How could anyone be fond of a cat?"

2. The farmer's wife saw the cat from a different point of view. Write two descriptive words that she uses to tell about the cat.

   a. _____   b. _____

3. Why do the mice and the farmer's wife feel differently about the cat?

   _____

4. Write two words from the story that Percy uses to describe mice.

   _____

5. What words does Percy use to describe how the new people in the house feel about mice?

   _____

6. What word does the farmer's wife use to describe the mice?

   _____

Name _____

Belling the Cat

Using Quotation Marks

Quotation marks show a speaker's exact words. The first word in a quotation is capitalized. The punctuation at the end of a quotation goes inside the quotation marks.

Add quotation marks to the following conversations to help show the speakers' exact words.

1. Leah has a good idea, but it is hard to carry out, said Percy. Who can think of a way to solve this dilemma?

2. What about a large loop of rope stretched between the chair and the table? suggested Agatha. When the cat walks by, we could pull on the rope and close the loop.

3. Do you think we could find a rope? Who will hang the loop between the chair and the table? asked Percy. There must be an easier way. We can't risk losing any more mousepower.

4. What a wonderful idea! The mice clapped in approval. Let's get to work on the collar.

The Day the Yam Talked

An Ashanti Folktale

Long ago, a farmer decided it was time to dig up the yams in his garden and take them to the marketplace in the village. He'd been busy with this and that and hadn't taken time to weed and care for the yams.

"Even so," he said to his wife, "the yams always grow well on their own."

The farmer went to the field and began to dig between the tangled vines.

A voice said, "Why have you waited so long to come to my field? You haven't watered or cared for me. Go away and leave me alone!"

"Who said that?" asked the farmer.

"It was the yam," answered the dog. "He's right, you know. You were lazy. Look at this field, covered with weeds and twisted vines."

The farmer didn't like the way the dog had talked to him. "I will tie you up, and you won't be able to follow me to market." The farmer cut a vine from the tree.

"You can leave me alone too," said the vine. "Hang me back on the tree."

The farmer dropped the vine on a rock. The rock said, "I want to feel the warm sun on my back. Get that vine away from me."

The farmer was afraid. He ran along the path toward the village to tell the chief what he had heard.

Soon he came to a fisherman who was catching fish in a basket trap. "Farmer, why are you running on such a hot day? Are you being chased by a lion or running after a hare?"

"It's not that at all. This morning a yam said, 'Go away and leave me alone.' My dog said, 'He's right, you know.' I cut a vine to tie up the dog, and the vine said, 'Hang me back on the tree.' I dropped the vine on a rock and the rock said, 'Get that vine away from me.'"

"I'm going to the village to tell the chief what I have heard," explained the farmer.

"No yam has ever talked to me," said the fisherman, not believing what the farmer said. "Go back to your farm and forget about it."

The fisherman's basket spoke up, "Finish the story. How long do I have to wait to hear the ending? Did the farmer take the vine off the rock?"

The fisherman dropped the basket and ran toward the village with the farmer. Soon the farmer and the fisherman came to a weaver who was carrying his cloth to the village.

"Why are you running so fast on such a hot day? Are you being chased by an elephant or are you trying to catch an antelope?"

"It's not that at all," said the farmer. "This morning a yam said, 'Go away and leave me alone.' My dog said, 'He's right, you know.' I cut a vine to tie up the dog, and the vine said, 'Hang me back on the tree.' I dropped the vine on a rock, and the rock said, 'Get that vine away from me.'"

"And then," said the fisherman, "my basket said, 'Did the farmer take the vine off the rock?'"

"We're going to the village to tell the chief what we have heard," explained the farmer.

"Who ever heard of a talking yam? Go back to your work," said the weaver.

The bundle of cloth said, "You'd run to the village too, if you had heard the yam."

The weaver dropped his cloth and ran after the farmer and the fisherman. Soon they came to a man swimming in the river.

"Why are you running when the sun is overhead? Are you being chased by a leopard or running after a goat?"

The three men told their stories.

The swimmer laughed. "Who ever heard of a talking yam? Go back to your work."

The river said, "A talking yam? You'd better run too."

Ghana

The swimmer ran after the others. They came to the village and bowed before the chief who was seated on the golden stool.

"Speak," said the chief.

"Oh, great chief," said the farmer, "this morning a yam said, 'Go away and leave me alone.' My dog said, 'He's right, you know.' I cut a vine to tie up the dog, and the vine said, 'Hang me back on the tree.' I dropped the vine on a rock and the rock said, 'Get that vine away from me.'"

The fisherman spoke. "My basket asked, 'Did the farmer take the vine off the rock?'"

"My bundle of cloth said, 'You'd run to the village too, if you heard a talking yam,'" said the weaver.

"The river said, 'You'd better run too,'" said the swimmer.

"How can you bother me with this silly talk?" said the chief. "Go back to your work before I punish all of you."

The men ran from the village.

"Imagine," said the chief's golden stool. "A yam that talks."

Questions about
The Day the Yam Talked

1. Why did the yam tell the farmer to go away?

   _____

2. Why didn't the farmer like what the dog said?

   _____

3. What did the vine want the farmer to do?

   _____

4. Why did the fisherman, the weaver, and the swimmer run to the village with the farmer?

   _____

   _____

5. Why didn't the chief believe the stories the men told?

   _____

6. Do you think the chief believed the men after he heard the golden stool talk? Explain your answer.

   _____

   _____

7. How would the story be different if the farmer had cared for the yams?

   _____

   _____

Name _____

The Day the Yam Talked

Vocabulary

1. Write each word below on the line next to its synonym. Use the clues in the story and the dictionary to help you.

tangled   alone   stool   punish   asked

a. _____ solitary

b. _____ cause discomfort to for some fault

c. _____ questioned

d. _____ intertwined, twisted

e. _____ a seat

2. Write each word below on the line next to its meaning. Use the clues in the story and the dictionary to help you.

weaver   yam   hare   twisted   vine   bundle   explained

a. _____ made the meaning clear

b. _____ a climbing, long-stemmed plant

c. _____ a rabbitlike animal

d. _____ a root that is eaten

e. _____ objects bound together

f. _____ a person who makes fabric or material

g. _____ not straight

3. Write sentences that tell about the story, using each of these words:

yams   marketplace   tangled   chief

_____

_____

_____

_____

The Day the Yam Talked

Personification

Sometimes authors give objects and animals human characteristics. This is called **personification**. In *The Day the Yam Talked* there are many nonhuman characters that talk.

Make a list of the nonhuman characters that talk in the story. Write them in the order they appear in the story.

1. _____   5. _____

2. _____   6. _____

3. _____   7. _____

4. _____   8. _____

Setting

The **setting** in a story is the place where the action happens. Under each setting given below, name the items that were personified.

The garden

_____

_____

Along the path

_____

_____

In the village

_____

_____

The Day the Yam Talked

Point of View

Select one talking object or animal from the story. Write about the object's or animal's life from its point of view. For example, the cloth might tell about being woven, bundled up, and taken to the market. It could tell about being made into clothing and what it sees on the way to the market, or describe what it sees at the market. The dog could talk about following his master around during the day. The river could talk about all the people and animals that come to the river, or its trip to the ocean.

_____

_____

_____

_____

_____

_____

_____

_____

_____

_____

_____

_____

_____

The Warrior and the Princess

The Mexican Legend of Ixtaccihuatl and Popocatepetl

In ancient times in the valley of Mexico, there lived a rich and powerful emperor. Colorful murals covered his palace. Jewels and brilliant quetzal feathers covered his crown. The treasure the emperor prized the most was his daughter, Ixtli. Her long, dark hair glistened like polished obsidian. Her eyes were a soft brown like the eyes of the deer that wandered in her garden. She was the most beautiful woman in the kingdom. Every young man who saw Ixtli wished to marry her, but no suitors pleased both the emperor and Ixtli.

One day Prince Popo, a great warrior, traveled from his neighboring kingdom to the valley to search for a wife. He saw Ixtli being carried to the marketplace on a litter. "She is as beautiful as people say," thought the prince. "But beauty alone is not enough. I can only love someone who has a kind and caring spirit."

Prince Popo disguised himself as a royal gardener so he could be near Ixtli to find out what she was really like. He watched her care for the animals in the garden. Ixtli often sent messengers with clothing and food to the poor people in the valley. Each day Popo fell more in love with her.

Finally, Popo could wait no longer. He knelt before Ixtli. "Forgive me, princess, I am not a gardener at all. I am Prince Popo from the mountain kingdom. I have worked in your garden to be near you. I have found that you are as kind as you are beautiful. I will love you forever."

Ixtli smiled at the young prince. She had fallen in love with this handsome gardener. She hadn't told anyone. She knew her father would never let her marry a commoner. But a prince! Surely he would agree to their marriage if it would bring her happiness.

Ixtli gave Popo the gold ring from her finger. "You must speak to my father. Show him my ring so he knows I have pledged my love to you."

"Oh, Princess, your love has made me happy. I will go to my kingdom to tell my people of your great beauty. Then I will return to claim your hand."

Ixtli waited for the young prince to visit her father. Day after day she watched for him. Months passed. Ixtli grew thin and pale. She worried about the prince. Had he been injured? Was he ill?

One afternoon as she sat by a window, one of her attendants ran into her room. "Prince Popo is here! He has come with a chest of treasures."

Ixtli ran to the visitor's room. "I thought you would never return," she said.

"I come from a poor mountain kingdom," answered the prince. "I could not return until I had treasures worthy of you. I have come today to ask your father to allow me to marry you."

"I will not hear of it!" stormed the emperor. "You are a prince of nothing. The one who marries my daughter must be worthy to rule my kingdom." Ixtli ran sobbing from the room.

Months passed. Ixtli pleaded with her father. Finally, seeing how unhappy his daughter was, he sent for the young prince.

"My daughter's happiness is important to me. I am willing to reconsider my decision if only to see her smile again. But first you must show me you are worthy of my daughter before I allow you to marry her," said the emperor. "You will be my messenger to all the kingdoms that surround our valley."

One day when Popo was carrying messages to a nearby kingdom, he saw soldiers marching toward the valley. He ran two days through the forests and mountains to warn the emperor. The emperor's troops hadn't fought battles for many years. Popo knew they would need a strong leader.

"I will command your soldiers," Popo told the emperor. "I have led my people against these same armies and defeated them."

"You have proven yourself a worthy messenger," the emperor said. "If you are a victorious warrior as well, you shall marry my daughter."

Popo and the emperor's soldiers fought the invaders for more than a year. When a messenger falsely reported that Popo had been killed, Ixtli died of grief.

The same day she died, Popo and his army of warriors returned. He bowed before the emperor. "There were many enemies, but we have won each battle. I will train every man in this kingdom so you will never be defeated."

The emperor, saddened by the death of Ixtli, placed his crown on Popo's head. "You have earned the kingdom, my son."

"I will accept the throne if I may marry Ixtli," said Popo.

The emperor led Popo to Ixtli's room. "She died this very day, thinking that you would never return."

Popo turned away from the emperor and picked up Ixtli. He carried her to the hills overlooking the valley. Holding a torch, he watched over her, hoping she would return to life. The snows came and covered the princess. Still Popo wouldn't leave her.

Today you can still see Popo and Ixtli on the hills overlooking the Valley of Mexico. The gods changed Ixtli into a snow-covered mountain called The Sleeping Woman. Popo, the brave and loyal warrior, became the smoking volcano that guards the mountain.

Name _____

Questions about
The Warrior and the Princess

1. Why was Ixtli unmarried?

   _____

   _____

2. Why did Popo pretend to be a gardener?

   _____

3. What did the prince find out about Ixtli while he was posing as a gardener?

   _____

   _____

4. Why did Popo wait so long to ask the emperor if he could marry Ixtli?

   _____

   _____

5. Why did the emperor refuse to allow Prince Popo to marry his daughter?

   _____

   _____

6. How could you tell that Ixtli truly loved Prince Popo?

   _____

   _____

7. Legends often explain the reason for the existence of something in the natural world. What does this legend explain?

   _____

   _____

Name _____

The Warrior and the Princess
Word Meaning

Fill in the blanks in the sentences using these words.

ancient   obsidian   quetzal   litter   disguised   bouquets

1. The black, glasslike _____ glistened in the sunlight.

2. The _____ story about the princess and the warrior takes place in Mexico.

3. Popo brought the princess _____ of flowers.

4. Four servants carried the king on a stretcher that was called a

_____.

5. The beautiful green feathers of the _____ bird were prized decorations.

6. Popo _____ himself as a royal gardener.

■ ■

Adjectives That Describe People

Read the list of words below that might be used to describe the personality and actions of the main characters in the story. Write each word beside the character or characters it describes. You may use a word more than once. Use a dictionary if you are unsure about a word's meaning.

beautiful	kind	brave	gentle	angry	caring	rich
despondent	strong	powerful	loyal	worthy	grieving	

Emperor _____

Princess Ixtli _____

Prince Popo _____

Name _____

The Warrior and the Princess
Similes

Similes are word pictures that compare one thing with something else. A simile gives the reader a clearer idea of what is being described. Similes use the connecting words *as* and *like*.

1. In the story, two similes are used to tell about Ixtli's beauty. The first one is written for you. Write the second one on the line.

   Her long, dark hair glistened like polished obsidian. _____

   _____

2. Write your own similes to complete these sentences.

   a. Prince Popo was brave like _____.

   b. When Popo asked to marry Ixtli, the emperor was as angry as _____

   _____.

   c. Ixtli was beautiful like _____.

3. There are many similes that describe something by comparing it to an animal that possesses a particular trait. Complete each of the similes below with the name of an animal.

   sly like a _____   as hungry as a _____

   as quick as a _____   as stubborn as a _____

   tall like a _____   walked like an _____

   as soft as a _____   worked like a _____

   as busy as a _____   as meek as a _____

   as strong as an _____   as quiet as a _____

Name _____

The Warrior and the Princess

Crossword Puzzle

Use these words from the story to complete the crossword puzzle.

murals   torch
brilliant   worthy
defeated   legend
warrior   valley
grief   Popo
Ixtli   search
suitors
pledged
victorious
injured
attendants
permission
commoner
emperor

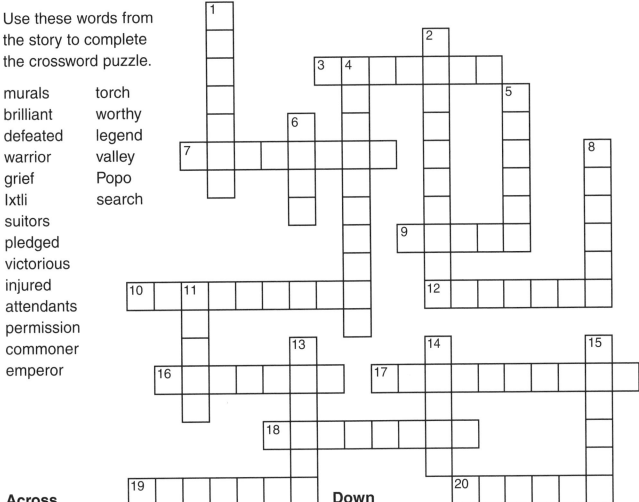

Across

3. a soldier
7. a person without the title of a noble
9. a carried, flaming stick
10. shining
12. men who give attention to women hoping they will agree to marriage
16. vowed, promised
17. approval to do something
18. overthrown; on the losing side
19. wounded or hurt
20. a lower, bowl-like area surrounded by hills or mountains

Down

1. a ruler over a vast area
2. having won a war or a contest
4. people who serve the royal family
5. to look for
6. the prince who became the volcano
8. large paintings on walls
11. the princess who became The Sleeping Woman mountain
13. a story that is told for a long period of time to explain something that happened
14. great sadness
15. deserving

The Fox and the Crow

An Adapted Fable

The crow ruffled his feathers and strutted up and down on the branch of his favorite tree. It was dinnertime. No berries, bugs, or worms would do. The other crows could eat that common food.

The crow flew from the branch and circled over a nearby farm. Being a very clever thief, he decided to steal a special delicacy for his dinner. He landed near the farmer's barn. Inside on a shelf were bricks of aging cheese. The crow pranced around the cheese. He eyed each brick. Every now and then he stopped and took a peck at one of the cheeses. Finally, near the end of the row, he found the perfect flavor. The crow heard the farmer's wife singing in the kitchen. He could see the farmer milking a cow in another part of the barn.

The crow pulled off a large piece of cheese. The noise from his flapping wings brought the farmer out. He chased after the crow, waving his arms and shouting. The crow flew above the trees in the orchard. The farmer couldn't catch him.

The crow flew back to the tree limb. It wouldn't do to eat a treat like this right away. He decided to wait until the rest of the flock was there so they could envy his tasty treasure. They would return soon, arguing about who had found the most bugs and worms in the farmer's freshly plowed field. It would be worth the wait to show them the cheese and devour it in front of them.

From her hiding place, a fox spied the crow. "I shall have that tasty morsel for myself," she declared to her husband. "It would be a shame to waste such a treat on a crow. That bird thinks too well of himself. I've heard him boast about his skill as a thief to all the creatures in the forest. It will be easy to take his dinner away. Just watch what I can do."

The fox crept out of the thicket and sat under the tree. She looked up and smiled, showing all her teeth. "Ah, dear crow, I see you have outfoxed the farmer again. I have never encountered another thief as clever as you are. We foxes are thought to be the wiliest animals on earth. We can claim that title no longer. I predict, dear crow, that you will soon be king of the forest."

The crow moved his head from side to side to show off the cheese.

"You are as handsome as you are clever, friend crow. Your feathers glisten in the sunlight. I can see bright, iridescent shades of green and a rainbow of colors dancing on your wings. Your eyes sparkle like jewels as they search the world for treasures. How I would love to replace my feet with yours so I could sit in the tree and watch the world below me. In a few words, dear crow, there is no creature in the forest that can compare with you."

The crow flapped his wings and looked down at the fox. "I can see," continued the fox, "that you know I speak the truth. Believe me, dear crow, I cannot praise you enough. Many animals say the voice of the crow is the most unpleasant sound they have ever heard. Indeed, they are mistaken. How could any animal as handsome and as talented as you make unappealing sounds?"

The crow nodded his head in agreement.

"I don't wish to interrupt your dinner—not for one minute. However, as a favor to this poor fox who will never be able to imitate your soothing, melodious tones, please sing a few notes. Every creature in the forest will enjoy your musical talent. You could serenade us with a long concert or enrich our lives with a trilling lullaby. I foresee a great musical future for you."

The crow was pleased to hear the fox's flattering words.

"Well," said the fox. "Will you sing for us, dear crow?"

"How can I refuse a great admirer like the fox?" thought the crow.

The crow opened his beak for the first caw of his song. The cheese fell to the ground and was gobbled up by the fox. A sad and hungry crow watched the fox disappear into the thicket.

Questions about
The Fox and the Crow

1. Why didn't the crow wish to eat berries, bugs, or worms?

   _____

2. How did the crow decide which piece of cheese to steal?

   _____

3. Why didn't the crow eat the cheese right away?

   _____

4. Why do you think the crow believed the fox?

   _____

   _____

5. The fox praised the crow excessively and was not truthful in her praise. What is a word that means "to praise too much"? (Hint: It begins with the same blend as *fly.*)

   _____

6. The fox said that the crow thought too well of himself. What is a word that names someone who behaves like the crow?

   _____

7. Every fable has a moral or lesson. Write a moral for *The Fox and the Crow*. Explain why you selected this moral.

   _____

   _____

   _____

Name _____

The Fox and the Crow
Vocabulary

1. Find words in the story to complete the following descriptions about the crow.

   a. The crow's feathers were an _____ shade of green.

   b. The crow's eyes were like _____.

   c. The crow's feathers _____ in the sunlight.

   d. A _____ of colors danced across the crow's wings.

   e. You are a _____ thief.

2. There are many words about music in the story. Write at least six of them on these lines.

   _____   _____

   _____   _____

   _____   _____

3. Use story clues and a dictionary to match the words below with their meanings. Write the letter of the word in front of its definition.

   a. melodious   _____ a musical performance

   b. trilling   _____ speaking too favorably about someone

   c. delicacy   _____ to eat up

   d. ordinary   _____ to stop someone who is speaking

   e. serenade   _____ sweet sounding

   f. orchard   _____ a rapid movement of the voice

   g. devour   _____ a special treat

   h. boast   _____ a field of planted fruit or nut trees

   i. interrupt   _____ common

   j. flattering   _____ to brag

   k. wily   _____ cunning, clever

Name _____

The Fox and the Crow

Prefixes

Prefixes are letter groups added before a base (root) word that can change the meaning of a word. Knowing the meaning of a prefix can help you understand what a word means.

Here is a list of prefixes and their meanings:

en	to make or become, put into
re	again
un	opposite of, not
pre	before
mis	bad, wrong
fore	front, before
dis	opposite of, not

Use the definitions of the prefixes to write the meanings of the words below. The first one has been done for you. You may need to use the dictionary.

1. predict: _to tell what will happen before it takes place_____

2. foresee: _____

3. enrich: _____

4. enjoy: _____

5. unappealing: _____

6. prearrange: _____

7. unable: _____

8. replace: _____

9. return: _____

10. forewarn: _____

11. disappear: _____

12. misjudge: _____

13. disagree: _____

14. misfortune: _____

Name _____

The Fox and the Crow
Write a Fable

Read all the directions for 1 through 6 before you begin to write.

1. Read the following shortened version of the fable about the ant and the grasshopper.

2. On another paper, write the story in your own words. Include the conversation between the ant and the grasshopper.

3. Remember to use quotation marks. Reread the story about the fox and the crow to see how conversations are punctuated.

4. Do you think the ant should help the grasshopper? Write your own ending to the story to show what happens to the grasshopper.

5. Add a moral to your story.

6. Illustrate the story.

The Ant and the Grasshopper

   An ant had worked very hard all summer and fall gathering food for the winter. He stored his food in his underground house. A hungry grasshopper, knowing that winter snow would soon cover the ground with snow, asked the ant to give him food. The grasshopper had been busy all summer and fall chirping and hopping and hadn't had time to prepare for winter.

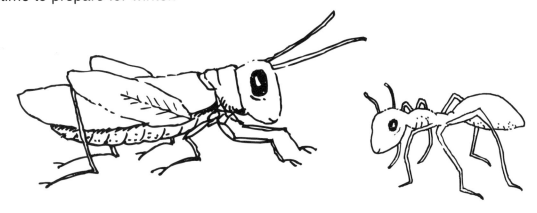

The Missing Grocery Money

Margaret emptied the shoe box on the floor. It was a lot of money, $38.27, and almost enough. Maybe by Monday she'd have enough to buy the bicycle at the Almost New store.

Life was different in Parktown than it had been in the city. All her new friends had bikes. If she didn't get a bike before school was out, the girls in her sixth grade class would forget all about her. During vacation, they planned to meet at each other's houses even though they lived in different sections of town. They talked about bike trips and swimming at the pool. It would be a long, boring summer without a bike.

In Margaret's family, there wasn't enough money left over for extras like bicycles. That's why Margaret started a pet-sitting business and ran errands.

Margaret wheeled her brother's old wagon out of the garage and headed for Mrs. Perry's house. When she rang the doorbell, Mrs. Perry answered with her usual greeting, "Well, hello. Here's my little Miss Sunshine right on time. You are so dependable."

Margaret was glad there wasn't anyone else around to hear the part about Miss Sunshine.

"Let's see," Mrs. Perry said, "I put the envelope on the table, I think. No, here it is on the kitchen counter."

"Be back soon, Mrs. Perry." Margaret waved and started down the walk.

"I'll wait for that smile, Miss Sunshine. It will brighten up my whole day!"

Even though the "Sunshine" part was embarrassing, Margaret was glad she could be helpful. Mrs. Perry could only get around with a walker.

Margaret put the envelope in her jacket pocket and walked quickly down the street. When she came to the park, she saw Gina and Alice sitting at the picnic table.

"Hey, Mag," Gina called. "Alice's mom made cookies. I brought punch. Come on. There's enough for the whole world. Gobble up a handful. We're having an eat-'til-you-burst tournament."

"What's with the wagon?" Alice asked.

"On Saturdays I pick up Mrs. Perry's medicine and groceries. She can't get out. I can't stay very long. She expects me back early."

"We're going to my house anyway," said Gina. "You could come after you help Mrs. Perry."

"I promised the Smiths I'd sit with their dog while they're gone. I'm going to read a book or watch TV over there so he has company this afternoon."

"People really trust you to help. Nobody asks me to do anything," said Alice. "It must make you feel great to volunteer."

Margaret nodded. For the first time she thought about being paid for helping Mrs. Perry. Maybe she should do it for nothing—"volunteer" like Alice said. After she got the bicycle, she might try it. The sun was out now, so she took off her jacket. "I'm on my way. See you Monday."

A block away, Gina caught up with her. "Hey, Mag. I found this by the table. Is it yours?" Gina handed her Mrs. Perry's envelope.

"You saved my life," Margaret said. "Mrs. Perry's check for the medicine and the grocery money are inside. Thanks."

At the supermarket a clerk packed Mrs. Perry's order in the wagon. Margaret looked inside the envelope. There was just the check for the pharmacy. "I don't know what happened. I must have lost the money."

"I can keep everything in the refrigerator until you come back with more money," said the clerk. "The manager isn't here, so I can't let the groceries go unless I have a payment."

Margaret searched for the money on her way back to the park. She looked carefully around the picnic table, but she didn't find anything. "Dependable Margaret!" she said sarcastically.

Margaret stopped at her house. What could she do? Mrs. Perry might not have any more money. Even worse, she might think Margaret had taken her money and kept it.

Margaret sat on her bed. She could say it was Mrs. Perry's fault because she hadn't sealed the envelope. That wouldn't be fair. Margaret knew if she had gone right to the supermarket, it wouldn't have happened. There was only one good solution. Margaret emptied her own money into her purse, went back to the market, and picked up the groceries. Feeling pretty glum, she wheeled the wagon to Mrs. Perry's.

"Well, Miss Sunshine, am I glad to see you! How did you manage to get the groceries? I found the grocery money in this envelope on the TV. I must have put the check for the medicine and the grocery money in different envelopes. Do you have time to take the money by the market?"

"You don't have to pay anything. I thought I'd lost the money," Margaret said. "So I paid for the groceries with the money I'd saved. I didn't want you to think I had taken it."

"Miss Sunshine, I know you'd never do that. There's enough in the envelope to pay you for the groceries and a little bit extra. You are such a thoughtful girl. I don't know what I'd do without you." Mrs. Perry gave Margaret a hug.

Questions about
The Missing Grocery Money

1. Why did Margaret want a bicycle?

   _____

2. What did Margaret do to earn money?

   _____

3. Why couldn't Mrs. Perry go to the supermarket and the pharmacy?

   _____

4. What is the difference between a person who volunteers to help and one who earns money for helping?

   _____

   _____

5. Why was Margaret's decision to pay for the groceries with her own money a difficult one?

   _____

   _____

6. Do you think Margaret should have paid for the groceries with her own money? Explain your answer.

   _____

   _____

7. The author of this story may have had some lessons in mind. What lesson or lessons do you think Margaret learned?

   _____

   _____

   _____

Name _____

The Missing Grocery Money
Vocabulary

A. Replace the words under the lines with words from this list.

guests	money	separate	repair
relied	considerate	discovered	uninteresting

1. She'd have to _____ it.
   (fix)

2. It would be an _____ summer.
   (boring)

3. There weren't many _____.
   (visitors)

4. I _____ this by the table.
   (found)

5. She _____ on Margaret.
   (depended)

6. She might not have extra _____.
   (cash)

7. Mrs. Perry said Margaret was _____.
   (thoughtful)

8. Mrs. Perry put the check and the money in _____ envelopes.
   (different)

B. Other characters in the story described Margaret's character. What did they say?

Mrs. Perry _____

Alice _____

The Missing Grocery Money
Suffixes

A. Suffixes are letter groups that are added to the end of a base (root) word. Some common suffixes are *ful, ment, ness, able, less, ly, er, ist,* and *en.* Add a suffix to the word under each line to correctly complete the sentence. (You may need to make some spelling changes.)

1. Alex was very _____.
(depend)

2. She finished _____.
(quick)

3. He took a _____ of peanuts.
(hand)

4. Mary finished her homework with _____ from her mother.
(encourage)

5. Adam was _____ and he dropped the vase.
(care)

6. The _____ plowed the field.
(farm)

7. Martin was a _____ in the piano contest.
(final)

8. Sally removed some of the packages from the donkey to _____ its load.
(light)

9. She felt great _____ when she saw her new bicycle.
(happy)

B. The following sentences are from the story. Underline the words with suffixes. Then circle the suffixes.

1. Her mom was always saying that happiness was helping others.

2. Margaret put the envelope in her jacket pocket and walked quickly down the sidewalk.

3. She'd rather be nameless.

4. Margaret was glad she could be helpful.

5. After the pharmacist gave Margaret the medicine, she wheeled the wagon to Mrs. Perry's house.

Name _____

The Missing Grocery Money

Summarizing

The following sentences summarize the story in a few words. Using your own words, write three more sentences to finish the summary.

1. Margaret took care of pets and ran errands so she could earn money for a bike.

2. When she went to the store to pick up Mrs. Perry's groceries there was no money in the envelope.

3. _____

4. _____

5. _____

6. Mrs. Perry told Margaret she hadn't given her the money.

■ ■

Find these words in the word search.

thoughtful
taken
pharmacist
payment
happiness
tournament
handful
dependable
brighten

D	C	E	D	M	L	K	B	R	I
E	T	P	Z	T	H	L	R	Q	U
P	H	A	R	M	A	C	I	S	T
E	O	Y	B	N	P	K	G	Z	O
N	U	M	S	S	P	I	H	O	U
D	G	E	B	K	I	L	T	T	R
A	H	N	T	Z	N	T	E	R	N
B	T	T	A	K	E	N	N	M	A
L	F	D	L	D	S	C	K	F	M
E	U	R	O	S	S	O	B	R	E
N	L	T	A	B	L	M	H	A	N
H	A	N	D	F	U	L	D	T	T

The One-Inch Boy

An Adaptation of a Japanese Folktale

In Japan, an old woman and an old man wished for a child to fill their days with happiness. One day the man found a basket by his doorway. Tucked snugly in the basket was a finger-size child. The man called to his wife, and together they brought the basket into the house.

"What shall we call this wonderful child?" asked the wife.

"He is our own One-Inch Boy," said the husband, "and that will be his name."

The father made tiny chairs, a table, and a bed for his son. The mother cooked grains of rice and put them in a bowl the husband had carved from wood. Each day, One-Inch Boy became stronger, but he never grew bigger.

Even though One-Inch Boy was very small, he was helpful. He crawled under the table and chairs and found whatever was lost. He brought in blades of grass that could be dried and woven into mats and shoes. He rode on his father's shoulder when they went to the forest and pointed out fallen limbs that could be gathered for firewood.

Fifteen happy years went by. One day One-Inch Boy said to his parents, "I want to go to Kyoto to seek my fortune if you will allow it."

"How could we manage without you?" said his mother.

"Indeed," said his father. "You have given us great hope and joy."

Although his parents did not want One-Inch Boy to leave, he persisted. Finally they agreed. His father found a small lacquer bowl One-Inch Boy could use as a boat. His mother cut oars from chopsticks. She gave him a sewing-needle sword in a straw scabbard.

One-Inch Boy set off down the river in the bowl. He had food, his sword, and blessings from his parents. He promised to send for his parents as soon as he had made his fortune.

All went well during the first days of the journey. Then the weather changed. Tremendous winds and rain tossed the bowl from one side of the river to the other. One-Inch Boy tried to row to shore, but the waves were too high. A boat, much bigger than the bowl, bore down on One-Inch Boy. The waves made by the boat swamped the bowl, and One-Inch Boy was sure he would drown. "Help! Help!" he called out. When he had given up hope, a large hand pulled him from his boat.

"What is this?" the boatman cried out, "A boy no bigger than my finger? What are you doing on this dangerous river?"

"I was on my way to Kyoto to seek my fortune," One-Inch Boy said.

"What a coincidence," said the boatman. "I, too, was on my way to Kyoto to sell a load of wood. Come with me, and we shall go to the city together."

One-Inch Boy was very grateful. The long ride in the bowl had been very tiring. As thanks to the boatman, One-Inch Boy mended the net bag used for carrying the wood.

In Kyoto, he bid the boatman good-bye and set out to see the city. Before long, he came to a beautiful palace. One-Inch Boy easily slipped through the spaces in the iron fence and pounded on the palace doors.

"Noble lord, can you give me shelter while I seek my fortune?" he called.

A great man dressed in silk robes opened the doors and looked around him. "I thought I heard someone, but there is no one."

"Down here, good sir. I will serve you well for food and a place to stay."

The great man picked up One-Inch Boy. "Well, you have courage and you ask little for your services. Stay here with me if you will."

One-Inch Boy thanked the great man, and made himself at home. Everyone in the household marveled at his size. They gave him all he wished for.

On a spring afternoon, the noble's daughter carried One-Inch Boy on a walk. Her guards and ladies-in-waiting accompanied them. As they passed by a dense forest, an ogre roared from his hiding place behind the trees. He grabbed the noble's daughter. Her ladies-in-waiting fled and so did the guards. One-Inch Boy spoke. "Leave this beautiful lady alone, or you shall feel my sword." One-Inch Boy unsheathed his sword and struck the ogre.

The ogre laughed. "Not much of a meal, but it will do until I find something else to eat." He scooped up One-Inch Boy and swallowed him.

One-Inch Boy stabbed the inside of the ogre's stomach with his sword. The ogre screamed. He let go of the noble's daughter, and she ran to the palace.

One-Inch Boy climbed up the inside of the ogre, tickling and scratching the beast. When he reached the ogre's mouth, the creature sneezed, and One-Inch Boy flew out. As the wounded ogre whirled to run back into the forest, he dropped his charmed necklace on the ground. One-Inch Boy put the charm around his neck. Then he made a wish. Immediately, he was transformed into a tall, handsome nobleman.

In return for saving his daughter, the great lord in the palace offered One-Inch Boy half of his lands. His daughter happily agreed to marry One-Inch Boy. As he had promised, One-Inch Boy sent for his parents. They all lived happily the rest of their years.

Questions about
The One-Inch Boy

1. Despite his tiny size, what things was One-Inch Boy able to do?

   _____

   _____

2. What things would One-Inch Boy not have been able to do?

   _____

   _____

3. Describe One-Inch Boy's boat and equipment.

   _____

   _____

   _____

4. Why did One-Inch Boy want to go to Kyoto?

   _____

5. How did One-Inch Boy's size help him get what he wanted?

   _____

   _____

6. What reward did the noble give One-Inch Boy?

   _____

7. What promise did One-Inch Boy keep?

   _____

Name _____

The One-Inch Boy
Vocabulary

A. Write each word below on the line in front of its definition.

scabbard   charm   ogre   dense   miniature

ancient   persisted   lacquer   journey

1. _____ a special object that is said to bring good luck

2. _____ a sheath or a holder for a sword

3. _____ thick

4. _____ very old, long ago

5. _____ a monster

6. _____ a very small object

7. _____ a trip

8. _____ did not give up

9. _____ a highly polished coating covering wood

B. Choose the correct word to complete each sentence.

fortune   tremendous   unsheathed   coincidence   marveled

1. The knight _____ his sword and rode toward the palace.

2. He _____ at the magnificent murals on the ancient walls.

3. He left home to seek his _____ and learned that friends are more valuable than gold.

4. It was a _____ that both of the travelers were going to the same city.

5. A _____ storm flooded the town.

The One-Inch Boy

Drawing Conclusions

Sometimes an author does not explain everything. The reader must draw conclusions by putting together information. Read this paragraph.

> Felicia shuffled up the street toward her house. She could barely put one foot in front of the other. It took an enormous effort to climb the flight of stairs to her bedroom. She collapsed on the bed. A 10-kilometer race was too long.

The paragraph did not use the words *tired* or *exhausted*, but you knew how Felicia felt by the way she acted. The paragraph did not exactly say why Felicia felt as she did, but you could tell that she had just run a race. You **drew conclusions** based on the information in the paragraph.

What conclusions can you draw from these events in *The One-Inch Boy*?

1. One-Inch Boy crawled under the furniture to find lost items. He brought in blades of grass for weaving.

   _____

2. One-Inch Boy's father created a boat for him. His mother made oars and a sword.

   _____

3. The boatman pulled One-Inch Boy to safety and gave him a ride to Kyoto.

   _____

4. People in the noble's house gave One-Inch Boy whatever he wanted. The daughter carried him on walks.

   _____

5. One-Inch Boy yelled at the ogre and stabbed him in the stomach.

   _____

6. The noble gave One-Inch Boy half of his lands and his daughter's hand in marriage.

   _____

Name _____

The One-Inch Boy

Sequencing

Events from the story are given below. Number them in the order in which they happened. The first event in each part is numbered for you.

Part 1

_____ One-Inch Boy set off down the river in his bowl.

_1_ The old man found One-Inch Boy near his doorway.

_____ The bowl was flooded in the storm.

_____ One-Inch Boy helped his parents.

_____ The boatman rescued One-Inch Boy and took him to Kyoto.

Part 2

_____ One-Inch Boy made a wish with the ogre's charm and he grew tall.

_____ After the ogre sneezed and One-Inch Boy was free, the ogre fled.

_6_ He asked the great lord for food and shelter in return for his services.

_____ The ogre swallowed One-Inch Boy.

_____ One-Inch Boy fought inside the ogre.

Part 3

_____ One-Inch Boy sent for his parents.

_11_ The noble rewarded One-Inch Boy with half of his lands.

_____ The noble's daughter agreed to marry One-Inch Boy.

The Contest

It all began when a magician proclaimed that he, being the wisest person in the land, should be the next governor. No one cared to argue with the magician, for he might turn you into a pig or even a flowerpot if he wished. It was fearfully agreed that the magician would be governor and there was nothing the people could say. That is, until the milkmaid spoke to the laundress.

"That magician is a fraud," she said. "He can't change a frog into a prince or a caterpillar into a butterfly. As for smart, I declare, my cow is smarter than someone who loses his spectacles when they are on his nose. He can't even remember to put on his shoes before he goes outside."

Now that information would have stopped right there if it hadn't been for the shoemaker who overheard the whole conversation. "Did you hear what the milkmaid said this morning?" he asked the blacksmith. "The milkmaid says the magician will change us all into frogs if he becomes governor, and furthermore, he is not as smart as her cow."

When the innkeeper and his wife came for their horse, the blacksmith said, "Did you hear what the milkmaid said this morning?"

The innkeeper and his wife had been busy preparing breakfast for travelers. It upset them to find out there was news they didn't know. They prided themselves on knowing everything. When the villagers wanted to hear the latest gossip, they stopped at the inn for a hot bowl of soup. If the innkeeper and his wife had nothing to report, they made up something.

"Well," continued the blacksmith, "the milkmaid said that the magician was a frog, and she was smarter than he was." With his pounding and clanging all day, the blacksmith seldom heard anything the way it was said.

Before the day was out, everyone knew that the milkmaid had challenged the magician to a contest to see who was the smarter of the two. The winner would be governor. The judges were the village teacher, the carpenter, and the seamstress.

The magician was incensed that he had to compete with a milkmaid, but his ambition to become governor was strong, so he accepted the conditions.

The good-natured milkmaid was surprised to learn that she was a candidate for governor. But if the people wanted her wisdom, who was she to say she wouldn't share it.

On Wednesday, when the sun was directly overhead, all the people from the countryside and the village came to the square.

The judges took their places on the steps of the palace. They looked solemn and elegant in the long black robes. The magician stood barefoot in front of the judges. The milkmaid, waving to the crowd, rode up on a cow. She hopped down and bowed to the judges.

The first questions were simple ones like how many legs does an octopus have, or what is the name of your mother. Then a farmer asked, "Magician, I've always wondered where the center of the earth is."

"Well, it would seem to me," the magician stopped and thumbed through his notebooks. "I think it must be in the middle of the sea or somewhere."

The milkmaid smiled. "The center of the earth is, of course, right here, under the magician's bare feet. There can be no doubt."

"Preposterous!" screamed the magician.

"If you doubt my word, dear magician," the milkmaid said, "take a string and measure around the earth from where you stand. If your feet are not right on the center of the earth, even an inch off, then you will win."

Now the magician knew he could not do this and prove her right or wrong. He called for the next question.

"I would ask, how many stars are in the sky?" said the baker.

"How should I, or anyone else, know that answer," said the magician. "I would say 27, give or take one or two."

"You are wrong again," said the milkmaid. "There are as many stars in the sky as there are hairs in the magician's beard. I will pull the hairs out one at a time and count them while the magician counts the stars. If the number is the same, then you will know I am right." The magician screamed as she pulled the hairs from his beard. Even if the contest had been at night, he couldn't count stars while she took his beard apart.

"Stop! Stop!" he yelled.

"When you agree that I have answered the question correctly," replied the milkmaid, "I shall stop."

"I agree," said the magician.

A small child spoke. "I want to know, how do you measure all the water in the sea?"

"It's easy to do," said the milkmaid. "Just ask the magician to stop all the water from the rivers flowing into the sea. Then you count the milk pails you can fill with sea water."

"Ridiculous!" shouted the magician. "I can't do that. How absurd!"

"Do you have a better answer?" asked the milkmaid.

"Of course not," he argued. "No one does."

"Then," said the milkmaid, "let the judges choose the next governor."

In minutes the milkmaid was robed and seated on the governor's chair. The magician was so angry he screamed and stamped his feet. For the first time his magic tricks worked. He turned into a toad.

Questions about
The Contest

1. Why did the magician think he should be governor?

    _____

2. Why didn't the people disagree with the magician?

    _____

3. Why did the milkmaid think the magician was a fraud?

    _____

    _____

4. The conversation between the milkmaid and the laundress was passed on to a number of other people. What happened as the conversation was told over and over? What was the end result?

    _____

    _____

5. Why did the milkmaid agree to the contest?

    _____

6. What statement did the milkmaid make about the magician at the beginning of the story that came true later on?

    _____

    _____

7. Do you think the milkmaid should have been the next governor? Explain your answer.

    _____

    _____

Name _____

The Contest
Vocabulary

1. A number of occupations were mentioned in the story. Write each occupation next to its description.

farmer	milkmaid	innkeepers	magician	teacher	blacksmith	baker
laundress	governor	seamstress	carpenter	shoemaker	town crier	judges

a. _____ a person in charge of land and people

b. _____ someone who does magic tricks

c. _____ a person who mends and makes footwear

d. _____ a person who makes horseshoes and shoes horses

e. _____ people who provide food and rooms for sleeping
for travelers

f. _____ a female person who milks cows or works in a dairy

g. _____ a person who makes bread and pastries

h. _____ a person who sews clothing

i. _____ people who decide who is the winner in a contest

j. _____ a person who shouts out the news in the street

k. _____ a person who helps students learn

l. _____ a person in the country who plants, cares for, and
harvests crops

m. _____ a person who builds objects with wood

n. _____ a female person who washes clothes

2. Write the occupations that are compound words. _____

_____

3. Write the two adjectives used to describe the judges.

_____   _____

Name _____

The Contest

Characterization

Write words and phrases that describe the magician and the milkmaid.
Then write a paragraph comparing the two characters.

Magician
easily confused

Milkmaid
quick-thinking

Both

_____

_____

_____

_____

_____

_____

_____

_____

_____

The Contest

Synonyms

Use these words from the story to complete the crossword puzzle.

Word Box				
solemn	preposterous	argue	fraud	wisdom
governor	candidate	judges	contest	elegant
challenge	gossip	conversation	absurd	

Across

1. applicant
7. imposter
8. talk
13. rumors
14. serious

Down

2. ridiculous
3. debate
4. ruler
5. dare
6. absurd
9. referees
10. intelligence
11. exquisite
12. competition

Name _____

Runner Up

Jordan was not going to win this time. Zach checked the laces on his shoes and stretched. He'd cut a few seconds off his time since last spring. He glanced at Jordan two lanes over. Jordan had won every race he'd ever entered. Zach had come close last spring in the meet against Elmhurst. He was two seconds behind Jordan. Today wasn't a meet or anything like that, but the coach would be making up his mind about the events and runners for the season.

The first meet was in two weeks. Zach's granddad was coming from Wisconsin to see him run. Grandpa Morgan had been a track star. He'd won lots of medals and he even ran in the Olympics once. He was always telling his friends about Zach and how his grandson was going to the Olympics one day. It wouldn't be good enough to come in second with Grandpa Morgan watching. Besides, he'd told Grandpa Morgan he was the best runner on the team.

The flag went down, and Zach flew down the track. He was out in front where he wanted to be. At the halfway mark he knew someone else was moving up, but no one passed him. Three-quarters of the way around, and there was someone else pushing for the lead. It had to be Jordan. Zach had pressed so hard to be in front that he didn't have enough energy to hold the lead if someone challenged him. Even so, no one was passing him up. If he could hold on, maybe Jordan wouldn't be able to keep the pace. Zach's body ached, but he didn't slow down. The other runner made his move and crossed the finish line in front of Zach. The runners gradually slowed down. Zach moved to the bleachers and wiped his face with a damp towel.

"Whoa," said a voice behind him. "Great race, buddy. Thanks for tiring out the other runners with that fast start. It made winning a lot easier."

Zach turned to see Jordan with a grin on his face. "Save a little speed for the last half and maybe you'll be in front of me next time. That is, if I'm not so far ahead you can't catch me."

Zach felt angry inside, but he tried not to show it. Whenever Jordan wins, Zach thought, he's got to rub it in and tell me how I should have run. It was even worse than that. Zach knew Jordan was right. If he'd paced himself and stayed back, he could have taken the lead toward the end with a burst of speed. "Thanks," Zach said when he had his breath and his temper under control, "I'll keep that in mind."

For the first time, Zach was glad Jordan was the center of attention. The other runners crowded around him. Their conversation was over, and he didn't have to congratulate Jordan on running a great race.

The next two weeks, Zach tried holding back, but somehow it didn't work for him. He had to head out at the beginning of the race or he stayed way back the whole race. Jordan kept reminding him. "Don't worry about it, Zach, buddy, I can coast in this way. With a first and second there'll be more points on the board for Bennington."

The coach put both Zach and Jordan on the relay team. "Keep it fast," he said, "but not so fast you use up energy for the big race. With both of you on the team, just think of it as a warm-up. Zach, watch how Jordan handles it. He was on the relay team last year. Remember, we need the points, not a record."

Even though Zach didn't like having Jordan around, he did like running more than anything else. Grandpa Morgan said the great thing about running was that you were competing with yourself. You kept trying to better your record each time you ran. I guess he never had to worry about someone else, Zach thought. He was the one who always won—just like Jordan.

When Grandpa Morgan came, he and Zach went running in the morning before school. Grandpa Morgan told Zach about some of his races and the Olympics. "Your last two years in high school, you can stay with me," Grandpa Morgan said. "I know a great coach—me. I'll have you ready for college and the Olympics by the time you graduate," he said.

Zach wanted to run in the Olympics, but he wasn't sure Grandpa Morgan would think he was good enough when he saw Jordan finish first.

On the day of the meet, Grandpa Morgan and Zach were up early before anyone else. As they ate breakfast, Grandpa Morgan talked about running.

"Gramps," Zach interrupted, "I have to tell you this." Zachary had thought about what he should say for the last week. He decided to tell the truth even if it meant Grandpa Morgan wouldn't have anything more to do with him. "I'm not the best on the team," Zach continued. "I know I talk like I am sometimes. Jordan has never lost the mile. I'm not as good as you were."

"There's one rule about running, Zach. No matter how fast your feet fly, there's always someone who can cross the finish line in front of you. I won lots of races, but I lost some too. I don't have any Olympic medals, even though I was there. Sure, I hope you'll take up where I left off, if that's what you want. But I want you to know that even if you come in next to last, you're still the greatest grandkid I could ever have. Running was my whole life for so long, I don't have too much else to talk about. It's time I stopped talking about running and learned about something else. After the meet we'll go out to dinner, and you can tell me about the rest of your life. Is there a good movie we could take in too?"

Questions about *Runner Up*

1. How did Zach feel about Jordan? Why?

   _____

   _____

2. Why did Zach lose the race?

   _____

   _____

3. Why did Zach think it was important to win the race at the first track meet of the year?

   _____

   _____

4. What did Grandpa Morgan think was the best thing about running?

   _____

   _____

5. What important truth about competition did Grandpa Morgan tell Zach?

   _____

   _____

6. Why do you think Grandpa Morgan changed his attitude about Zach's running?

   _____

   _____

Name _____

Runner Up

Vocabulary

Many words have different forms that are related. For example, *season* and *seasonal*.
In each section below, use a form of the same word to complete each sentence.

1. competitive–having a strong desire to succeed
   competition–a contest
   competitor–one who competes

   a. The winner of the local dance _____ would compete in the
      state contest.

   b. Marc was a _____ in the state bowling competition.

   c. Mary was very _____ in baseball.

2. congratulate–praise a person's accomplishments
   congratulations–expressions of pleasure about someone's good fortune

   a. He received _____ from the principal of the school for his
      science achievements.

   b. The coach said, "I want to _____ you for your outstanding

      performance today."

3. challenge–an invitation to compete in a contest; something that is difficult
   challenger–a competitor; the one who challenges
   challenging–difficult

   a. It was the most _____ race he had ever run.

   b. It was a _____ to complete his homework on time.

   c. Mel's _____ watched him warm up for the broad jump.

4. event–something that happens
   eventful–many events or results

   a. He was scheduled for the second _____ at the track meet.

   b. Saturday was an _____ day.

Runner Up

Multiple Meanings

A. A word can have more than one meaning. Match the words below with the meanings underlined in each sentence.

1. reduced   2. examined   3. moving in front of
4. marked   5. sliced   6. achieving the required standard

_____ Zach <u>checked</u> the laces on his shoes and stretched.

_____ Zach <u>checked</u> the correct answer on the answer sheet.

_____ He <u>cut</u> a few seconds off his time last spring.

_____ He <u>cut</u> his finger on the paper's edge.

_____ No one was <u>passing</u> him.

_____ No one was <u>passing</u> the course.

B. One word can be used in different ways. Tell whether the underlined word in each sentence is used as a noun or a verb.

1. Today wasn't a <u>meet</u> or anything like that. _____

2. Steve was anxious to <u>meet</u> his new roommate. _____

3. Zach had to <u>press</u> so hard to be in front that he didn't have enough energy to hold

   the lead if someone challenged him. _____

4. The newspaper was ready to go to <u>press</u>. _____

5. He had to head out at the beginning of the <u>race</u>. _____

6. Zach's granddad was coming to see him <u>race</u>. _____

C. Use the word _record_ as a verb in one sentence and as a noun in another sentence.

_____

_____

Name _____

Runner Up

Write Your Own Ending

Write a new ending to the story *Runner Up*. Tell what happened at Zach's first track meet of the year. Include what happened in the competition between Jordan and Zach. How did Zach feel about the results?

_____

_____

_____

_____

_____

_____

_____

_____

_____

_____

_____

_____

_____

_____

The Spring Swim

An Adapted Fable

Amy's mother had sent her to her grandmother's house on a nearby hillside to invite her to dinner and the party. Amy stayed for lunch with her grandmother. Then she hurried home so she could help her mother bake and frost her brother's birthday cake.

On the walk home, Amy saw signs of spring everywhere. The day was warm, and delicate yellow flowers waved in the breeze. Amy saw a small toy boat floating down a mountain stream. There was no one around. It must be a toy someone lost, she thought. My little brother Michael would like a boat like this. Amy didn't have a birthday present for him. This would be the perfect gift. He could play with the boat in the bathtub.

As she watched, the boat drifted into a logjam and was caught. Amy found a tree branch and tried to reach the boat with it. It wasn't quite long enough. She moved the trunk of a fallen tree into the stream. Slowly she balanced on the trunk and crawled toward the middle of the stream. She touched the boat with the branch and drew it toward her. It was almost within her reach. The tree wobbled and Amy adjusted her balance. The little boat drifted away. When Amy felt safe again, she reached for the boat with the limb and drew it toward her again. Finally, it was close to the end of the tree trunk. Amy inched out to the end of the tree. She reached for the boat and stuffed it into her pocket. When she started to crawl back toward the bank, she slipped off the tree and tumbled into the water.

The water in the middle of the stream was deep and icy from the melted winter snow. Amy tried to hold onto the tree, but her hands slipped off. The current was swift and she couldn't swim toward shore. She held onto a small rock poking out of the stream. She called out, "Help, the water is cold. I'm drowning!" If the rock broke loose, she would be swept downstream.

Amy kept calling as long as she could. No one answered. Amy was losing hope when she saw her neighbor standing on the bank of the stream.

"I declare," the woman scolded. "Amy, I thought you had more sense than to go swimming this time of year. What would your mother say if she could see you playing in the water on a cold day like this? Look at your wet clothes. The least you could have done is go home for your bathing suit. I dare say though, if someone had known what you were up to, they would have sent you to your room. And today's your baby brother's birthday. You should be home helping him celebrate. Some children just think of themselves. What a shame! I should give you a piece of my mind. I can't wait to tell your mother."

"Oh, please, dear neighbor, you can tell my mother, or anyone, what you like. Could you save me first and give me a lecture later? I can't tread water any longer. If you keep talking, I will drown and you'll have no one to scold. There are lots of tree limbs around. Hold on to the end of one, and let me hold the other. Then pull me out of the water."

The neighbor realized how foolish she had been. She offered Amy the end of a limb and pulled her to shore. Kindly, she wrapped the young girl in her cloak and the two of them hurried home. Her family would be very surprised to learn what had happened, Amy thought. There was no doubt in her mind that the neighbor would be very happy to tell her own side of the story. At least Amy had saved the boat so they would believe her version of the spring swim.

Lesson: There is a time to talk and a time to act.

Name _____

Questions about
The Spring Swim

1. List several of the signs of spring that Amy noticed while on her errand.

   _____

   _____

2. What tempted Amy to take a dangerous course of action?

   _____

   _____

3. After Amy fell in the water, what did she do to try to save herself?

   _____

   _____

4. Why do you think the neighbor scolded Amy?

   _____

   _____

   _____

5. What is your opinion of Amy's actions in this story? Give facts to support your opinion.

   _____

   _____

   _____

6. Explain what the lesson at the end of the fable means.

   _____

   _____

The Spring Swim

Vocabulary

A. Choose a word or words to answer each question.

scolded   version   I declare   inched   lecture   current   foolish   stuffed

1. What word means "one's own side of the story"? _____

2. What word means "spoke sharply to"? _____

3. Which words mean about the same as "I dare say"? _____

4. What word describes the way Amy moved on the tree? _____

5. What word describes how Amy put the boat in her pocket?

_____

6. What word does Amy use to describe the way the neighbor talks to her?

_____

7. What word describes the movement of water? _____

8. What word means "silly or stupid"? _____

B. Amy said that she couldn't tread water much longer. What does "tread water" mean?

_____

C. The neighbor says she should give Amy "a piece of her mind." What does that expression mean?

_____

Name _____

The Spring Swim

Creative Writing

Write about what happens when Amy returns home. Don't forget to include the mother, the neighbor, Amy, and her little brother in the scene.

_____

_____

_____

_____

_____

_____

_____

_____

_____

_____

_____

_____

_____

_____

_____

_____

_____

Name _____

The Spring Swim

Alphabetical Order

Write these words in alphabetical order. Then find and circle each word in the word search.

delicate   wobbled   adjusted   version   declare   balance   limb   current   Amy
neighbor   lecture   realized   scold   foolish   tread   cloak   surprised   drown

_____

_____

_____

_____

_____

_____

_____

_____

_____

_____

_____

_____

_____

_____

_____

_____

_____

_____

```
L M D U Q P Z R N L R L N R
D E C L A R E O O E F G K U
S U R P R I S E D C T V C V
A B D O L D C S F T R H L Z
A V E R S I O N O U E H O P
D N L A M Y L Z O R A W A N
J L I M B T D O L E D O K G
U D C S K O N E I G H B O R
S B A L A N C E S B X B L C
T Z T D R O W N H D R L Q D
E R E A L I Z E D J J E D T
D C U R R E N T R C N D M N
```

Kaleidoscope

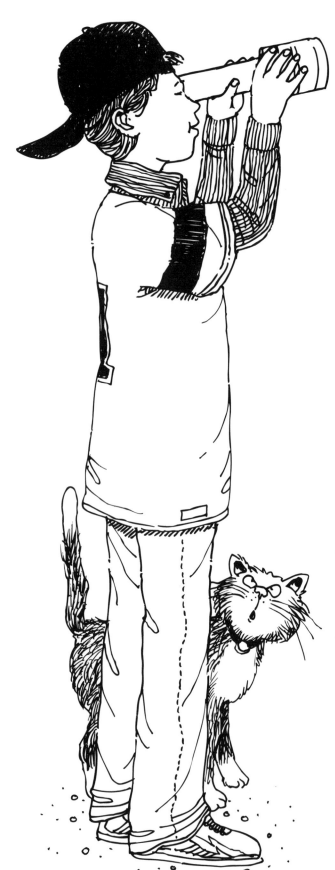

Mosaic bits of color
a sparkling crystal scene
golden summer sunsets
a splash of serpentine.

Geometric tree shapes
brown oak and evergreen
enchanting verdant forests
move across the screen.

Turning round, up then down
jumbled in between
a sky of dancing rainbows
with shades of tangerine.

A deep-jade flowing river
each fish a wishing star,
the crescent moon a sailing ship
it seems a bit bizarre.

Kaleidoscope will take me
to places near and far
imaginary kingdoms,
New York or Zanzibar.

I'll meet a gallant, flying steed
a prancing unicorn
with diamond mane and braided tail
and spiral, sapphire horn.

Castles, palace, desert tent
across a ruby sea
shining towers, golden bridge
shift and tumble free.

Painted creatures move about
beasts with emerald hair
dancing rabbits, purple sheep
they're spinning everywhere.

A flock of birds flying past
with glowing, patchwork wings
satin swans sail across
clear lakes and bubbling springs.

Roses, tulips, changing gems
how magical it seems
fantastic flower gardens
bright bouquets of dreams.

Kaleidoscope keeps turning
shapes form, then tumble on
treasured images, pictured jewels
how quickly they are gone.

Questions about *Kaleidoscope*

1. Some unusual animals are "seen" in the kaleidoscope. List and describe them.

   _____   _____

   _____   _____

   _____   _____

   _____   _____

2. What two specific locations are mentioned in the poem?

   _____   _____

3. A kaleidoscope can also take you to places not found on a map. What two words were used to describe such places?

   _____   _____

4. Would you say that the poet has a vivid imagination? Explain your answer.

   _____

   _____

   _____

5. What image in the poem was the most interesting to you?

   _____

Kaleidoscope

Adjectives

1. Words that describe nouns are called **adjectives**. Match each descriptive word from the poem with its definition.

   mosaic   verdant   spiral   crescent   bizarre   gallant   satin
   prancing braided geometric patchwork fantastic treasured

   a. _____ imaginary, terrific

   b. _____ a smooth shiny fabric

   c. _____ something that curves around to form circles

   d. _____ green with growing plants

   e. _____ highly valued

   f. _____ small, colored pieces forming a picture

   g. _____ odds and ends roughly put together

   h. _____ made of shapes such as squares, rectangles, etc.

   i. _____ three or more strands woven together

   j. _____ moving with high steps and leaps

   k. _____ name of a phase of the moon

   l. _____ brave and noble

   m. _____ odd, unusual

2. A number of words in the poem have to do with precious stones or minerals.
   Can you find at least six?

   _____ _____ _____

   _____ _____ _____

Kaleidoscope

Rhyming

In *Kaleidoscope*, the second and fourth words of each stanza **rhyme**—the ending sound of the words is the same.

1. The words *scene* and *serpentine* in the first stanza are not spelled the same, but they have the same ending sound. What other pairs of rhyming words in the poem have endings that **are not** spelled the same way? Write the words on these lines and underline the rhyming parts.

    a. _____   _____

    b. _____   _____

    c. _____   _____

2. Four sets of rhyming words in the poem have endings that **are** spelled the same. Write the pairs of words on these lines and underline the endings.

    a. _____   _____

    b. _____   _____

    c. _____   _____

    d. _____   _____

3. One rhyming ending is used six times in the poem. Another ending is used four times. Write these two groups of rhyming words.

    a. _____   b. _____

    _____   _____

    _____   _____

    _____   _____

    _____

Name _____

Kaleidoscope

Descriptive Language

1. Many of the images in the poem use color. Some of these images are realistic and others are imaginary. Classify the following images under one of the two headings listed below.

    purple sheep
    ruby sea
    golden bridge
    a deep-jade flowing river
    a flock of birds with glowing, patchwork wings
    brown oak and evergreen
    beasts with emerald hair
    golden summer sunsets

    Real   **Imaginary**

    _____   _____

    _____   _____

    _____   _____

    _____   _____

2. Select your favorite image from the poem. Write it here and tell what you like about this image.

    _____

    _____

    _____

Journey North

This letter might have been written by a young settler of early California.

April 10, 1781

My dear Grandfather and family,

I am writing this letter in the spring of the year 1781. More than five years have passed since we left New Spain. I am sending this letter so you will know about our journey and what has happened to us. My family and I are grateful that we enjoy good health. We know now that we will never be able to return to New Spain. The journey by land is too dangerous. Even the trip by sea is difficult and very long. My parents have asked me to caution you about joining us as we had agreed before we left. There is rich land here, but all that we have must be made or grown with our own hands. Our houses lack even small comforts. Sailing ships seldom come this way with supplies. My youngest brother, Pedro, was born here in Alta California. My other six brothers and sisters are busy helping my parents. Since I am thirteen now, I am responsible for the fields and care for the cattle while my father is guarding the mission and our communities.

I studied with Father Font, the Franciscan priest who accompanied us on the trip north. Learning to read and write during those difficult days gave me hope. Because of my good fortune, I am able to send you this letter about our journey.

Our leader, Juan Bautista de Anza, kept our caravan moving north in spite of hardships that you cannot imagine. He cared for those who became ill and gave cheer when our spirits and faith failed. Without him, we would have perished before we reached Alta California.

Traveling with the mules and cattle proved to be a challenge for our families. It was a major task to organize our caravan every day before we set out. We had to find food and water for the animals as we traveled to Monterey. We stopped many days so that the animals could eat and rest.

We were in good spirits the first few days of the trip, even though the winds and the desert crossing made our progress very slow. The hot summer days had passed, but the area was unpleasant. We found little water and grass for our animals.

A month later we reached the camp of a Pima chief on the banks of the Colorado River. The cold, bitter winter had made fording the river impossible. Many of us, who had never seen a river this wide, feared the crossing and would have returned to Mexico if we could. A narrow flow was found to the north, and the Pimas helped us cross. We exchanged gifts and were given fresh food from their gardens.

As we crossed the desert, the thick brush scratched our arms and legs. Dust and alkali were tossed about by icy winds. Our animals suffered. Some of them strayed and died. We finally found water. The animals drank until there was little left. We bundled grass for them and bottled the last of the water.

Our leader divided our animals into three herds so they would arrive at the water holes at different times. That way the water holes would have time to fill again between the herds. The ground froze, and more animals died. Somehow we survived. At one point the animals stampeded back to the last water hole. We could not stop them. Many froze to death.

On Christmas we camped by a village of native people. The cold and snow had surprised them too. They had nothing they could offer our animals or us. There was not even wood for fires.

Without horses for everyone, we could not continue. Our leader sent soldiers west to Mission San Gabriel. They were able to return with horses, but few supplies. We slowly made our way to the mission. Bandits stole some of our animals, and more horses died from the harsh weather. At San Gabriel we waited for supplies from another mission.

Even though our journey on to San Luis Obispo was uneventful, the long, difficult journey had made us despondent. Our spirits improved after we celebrated our safe arrival at the mission in San Luis Obispo. We gave thanks that we would soon be in Monterey.

If it had not been for the rain and mud, we would have reached our destination much sooner. We expected a town and shelter in Monterey, but we had to huddle in our tents during the storms. Because the settlement was new, there weren't enough buildings to shelter us. Even so, we gave thanks that we did not have to endure a longer journey. Some of our party would go farther north to a great bay, but our family stayed in Monterey. We looked for land and began the construction of our adobe house.

A galleon from Manila sets sail for New Spain tomorrow. When it will arrive in New Spain, I don't know. We have given the captain fresh spring water and vegetables for his table in return for delivering this letter. I have been told the letter will be sent north from the port of Acapulco by mule train with other mail and supplies. It may be a year before you receive this message, but it comes with great love from all of our family.

Antonio

Name _____

Questions about
Journey North

1. In what year did Antonio and his family leave New Spain?

   _____

2. Why did Antonio's parents discourage the rest of the family from coming
   to Alta California?

   _____

   _____

3. How does Antonio help his family?

   _____

   _____

4. Why do you think Antonio's parents asked him to write the letter?

   _____

5. Was Juan Bautista de Anza a good leader? Explain your answer.

   _____

   _____

6. List four hardships the expedition faced on their trip to Alta California.

   _____

   _____

   _____

7. Why will it take a long time for Antonio's grandfather to receive the letter?

   _____

   _____

Journey North

Vocabulary

A. Use these words from the story to complete the sentences below.

New Spain   caution   comforts   settlements   accompanied
caravan   progress   fording   alkali   strayed

1. The animals _____ from the camp during the night.

2. The travelers needed help in _____ the stream.

3. I must _____ you about joining us in Alta California.

4. The _____ took several hours to organize each day.

5. There are few _____ in Alta California.

6. The severe cold made the caravan's _____ very slow.

7. The desert dust and _____ blew in our faces and eyes.

8. Father Font _____ us on the journey.

9. Our journey from _____ to Monterey took 130 days.

10. We lived in small _____ and ranches near the missions.

B. Choose a word from this list to complete each sentence.

despondent   galleon   celebrated   survived
construction   exchanged   bitterly   challenge

1. The word *perished* means "died." The antonym for *perished* is _____.

2. A Spanish sailing ship was called a _____.

3. If you are building a house, it is under _____.

4. After days of travel and harsh conditions, the travelers became _____.

5. The weather turned _____ cold.

6. The travelers _____ their safe arrival.

7. They _____ gifts.

8. Caring for the animals on the difficult journey was a _____.

Journey North

Verbs

A **verb** is a word that can tell action. Write a sentence using the following verbs from the story. After you have written your sentences, compare each sentence with the way the verb is used in the story.

divided   suffered   stampeded   feared   camped   celebrated

_____

_____

_____

_____

_____

_____

_____

. . . .

Pronouns

Pronouns are words that take the place of nouns. Read the following sentences and phrases with pronouns. Review the story and write the noun that the pronoun replaces. For example, in the sentence *I am writing this letter*, the word *I* refers to *Antonio*.

1. When **it** will arrive in New Spain, I don't know. _____

2. **It** comes with great love from all of our family. _____

3. The cold and snow had surprised **them** too. _____

4. We could not stop **them**. _____

5. **We** know now that we will never be able to return to New Spain. _____

6. **They** were able to return with horses. _____

7. …were given fresh food from **their** gardens. _____

8. **He** cared for those who became ill. _____

Journey North

Sequence of Events

Number the events in the order in which they happened in the story.

_____ Our journey to San Luis Obispo was uneventful.

_____ Our leader divided our animals into three herds so they would arrive at the water holes at different times.

_____ A month later we reached the camp of a Pima chief on the banks of the Colorado River.

_____ On Christmas we camped by a village of native people.

_____ We expected a town and shelter in Monterey, but we had to huddle in our tents during the storms.

_____ We were in good spirits the first few days of our trip, even though the winds and the desert crossing made our progress very slow.

- -

Generalizing

1. Write a statement that explains why few people traveled to Alta California in the 1700s.

_____

_____

2. Write a statement that tells why people would brave the hardships to travel to Alta California.

_____

_____

The Race

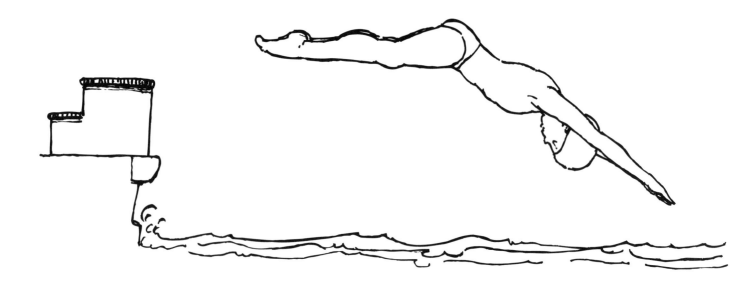

Mark shook out his arms and legs as he waited in the staging area. This was it. His heat was next. He had made the finals of the individual medley at the county swim meet. It hadn't been easy. He had spent the summer doing two-a-day workouts. But the conditioning had paid off and the extra lessons hadn't hurt either.

The announcer was introducing the swimmers. The names and faces were familiar. Mark had competed against most of them throughout the summer. There was Tony, his teammate, tall and lean as he flexed his arms; Jay, jumping up and down to keep his muscles loose; and Jeff, unwrapping his towel and sauntering forward. Mark heard his own name and stepped forward. He waved to the crowd before splashing some water on his face.

The announcer continued naming the rest of the swimmers, but Mark closed his eyes for a moment and thought about the upcoming race. He saw himself reaching for the wall. He could almost sense its rough surface on his fingertips. This was the moment he had been working for. One last glance around and he was ready.

The starter gave the signal and Mark stepped onto the block. The butterfly leg of the race was first.

"Take your marks."

Mark grabbed the edge of the starting block and rolled forward, ready for the gun. He was potential energy personified.

"Get set."

Mark tensed and the starter's gun cracked through the silence. The swimmers exploded off the blocks. Mark's body undulated as he flew down the lane in the churning water. His shoulders hunched forward. He threw his arms out of the water, forward, and back in again. His actions were automatic. He had practiced each movement over and over. The cup of his hands, the speed of his kick, and the position of his head were all important to his success.

The end of the pool appeared. Touch and push, streamline, dolphin kick, and Mark broke the surface on his back. His arms turned like the blades of a windmill stretching behind his head, slicing into the water, and pulling forward to begin again. The flags overhead signaled the end of the pool and Mark counted his strokes—2...3...4 and touch.

His fingers brushed the edge of the wall as he flipped over onto his stomach and pushed off. He reached, pulled, and glided as he began his breaststroke. His arms moved smoothly in a strong arc as his legs jerked in a frog kick.

There was only one lap to go—the freestyle. Eight swimmers pressed forward. Mark was tired, but his body was ready. He swam into the turn, touched the wall with both hands, and powered off the wall—a speeding missile bound for the finish. His arms stretched. His kick accelerated. He slid through the water. He reached for the wall.

It was just as he had imagined it. The rough texture bit into his fingertips. He raised his head and smiled. He was a winner!

Name _____

Questions about *The Race*

1. What kind of a race was Mark participating in?

   _____

2. How did he feel about the race?

   _____

3. The individual medley includes four strokes. Name them in the order they were swum in the story.

   _____

   _____

   _____

4. How did Mark know that he was coming to the end of the pool when he was doing the backstroke?

   _____

5. Do you think Mark won the race? Explain how the phrase "He was a winner" might apply to a different result.

   _____

   _____

6. Define "winner" in terms of your own experience.

   _____

   _____

Name _____

The Race
Vocabulary

A. Write the number of each word on the line in front of its definition.

1. medley   _____ stirring up violently

2. conditioning   _____ speeded up

3. sauntering   _____ a mixture

4. automatic   _____ instinctive, without conscious thought

5. churning   _____ strolling leisurely

6. accelerated   _____ preparation

B. Choose the meaning of each of these phrases from the story.

1. ...the conditioning had paid off...
    a. Mark would get money if he won the race.
    b. Mark's practice had gotten him to the finals.
    c. The other swimmers weren't in good shape.

2. He was potential energy personified.
    a. He was ready for action.
    b. He needed to get more energy.
    c. He was the winner.

3. The flags overhead signaled the end of the pool...
    a. The flags waved.
    b. The flags had writing on them.
    c. The flags were close to the end of the pool.

4. ...he flew down the lane...
    a. He was swimming fast.
    b. He lifted up out of the water.
    c. He went down the path.

Name _____

The Race

Action Verbs

The author of this story used many different action verbs and phrases to describe Mark's swimming. Reread the story and find 10 verbs and verb phrases that describe how he swam.

_____   _____

_____   _____

_____   _____

_____   _____

_____   _____

Think of different action verbs you could use to describe walking. Write five of them here. Then use them in sentences.

_____   _____

_____   _____

_____

_____

_____

_____

_____

_____

The Race

Figurative Language

Figurative language, which uses familiar words in unfamiliar ways, makes writing and reading more interesting. *The Race* includes examples of three common forms of figurative language—the simile, the metaphor, and personification.

| A **simile** is a figure of speech that makes a comparison using the words *like* or *as*. |

Write a simile used in *The Race*. What two things are being compared?

_____

_____

| A **metaphor** also makes comparisons, but without using the words *like* or *as*. A metaphor may say that one thing **is** another thing. |

Write a metaphor used in *The Race*. What two things are being compared?

_____

_____

| **Personification** means giving human characteristics to an idea or a thing. |

Write an example of personification used in *The Race*. What human characteristic was given to what thing?

_____

_____

Two Sisters

A Folktale

Once, not so long ago, two sisters inherited land from their father. The younger sister, Ella, received land that was hilly and rocky. The older one, Gretta, happily took over property with planted fields and orchards. There was even a stream near the orchard so she could water her plants and trees.

Ella didn't complain about her misfortune. The land was a gift, and she was grateful to have it. She set to work terracing and cultivating the hills. The work was hard, and she had to go to the river for water when there wasn't enough rain. But in a few years, her land produced twice the crops as her sister's.

Gretta enjoyed feeling important and busied herself with meetings in town. She took in the crops and gathered the fruit, but she didn't have time to prepare the ground for the next planting. In the spring, there were more weeds than carrots. She didn't prune the trees, so they lacked new growth and blossoms. Another year passed and there was even less to take to market.

Gretta watched her sister take cartloads of produce to the marketplace. She spied on her to see how she could manage so well with land that had never grown anything. One day she overheard Ella talking to a pear tree.

"Soon, dear tree, your magic blossoms will turn to fruit, and I will take your juicy pears to the marketplace where everyone will admire them."

Gretta confronted her sister. "That's it! I knew it. It's impossible to grow fruit and vegetables on this worthless land without magic. I will tell everyone your fruit is enchanted."

"Enchanting perhaps, dear sister, but not enchanted," Ella answered.

"Do you deny that you use magic to grow your trees and plants?" Gretta demanded.

"It is magical to see the blossoms and green plants sprout, I can't deny that," said Ella.

Gretta hurried home. That night she went to Ella's orchard. She dug the tiny tree from the ground and hurried home. The next day she planted the tree in her own orchard. "Now I have the

Read and Understand, Fiction • Grades 4–6 • EMC 748

magic tree," she said, "and everything will grow for me. My sister will have nothing at all." Gretta did not think to water the little tree, and it died as her other trees had.

Ella was sad to find her tree was missing, but she reasoned that if her sister learned to care for the tree, her orchards would grow again and she, too, would be prosperous.

Gretta was very angry now. "I don't know the magic words," she said to her cat. "I should have listened to what my sister said. I will find out what her magic is."

Gretta hid behind the trees in Ella's orchard. Ella saw Gretta's purple shoes and flowered hat poke out from behind the tree. She watered an apple tree and said loudly so Gretta could hear, "Dear tree, you have rewarded me with sweet fruit this year. So your magic will continue, I will give you water when your roots are dry and trim your branches when your leaves cloak the ground. Then you can work your magic and fill my baskets with fruit again."

Gretta waited until it was dark. In the moonlight she dug out the tree and dragged it to her orchard. She planted the tree in a large hole and watered it. When the air was cold and the tree's golden leaves blanketed the ground, she carefully trimmed the branches. The next spring, the tree was covered with blossoms. Gretta continued to water and care for the tree. Apples covered the tree, and Gretta proudly took baskets of fruit to the marketplace.

She waved at Ella, but she didn't stop to talk. That afternoon Ella came to Gretta's house with a cartload of young fruit trees. "Dear sister, now that you know my magic secret, I have come to help you replant your orchard."

"I did happen to hear your magic words," said Gretta. "I said them to the tree every day, and the tree grew baskets of apples."

"Words?" Ella said. "My magic is not words at all. My magic comes from two strong branches and sturdy roots that aren't planted in the ground. Without knowing it, you have discovered my real magic."

"What nonsense!" Gretta said. "I didn't see anything like that in your orchard. If I had, I would have taken it home with me and not had to work so hard."

"You weren't looking in the right place," Ella said. "Watch now and I will put those branches and roots to work." Ella began to dig holes and plant the trees. When she finished, she said, "These, you see, are my magic branches." Ella hugged her sister with her arms. "And my legs are my magic roots. I created my own magic, Gretta. You have the same magic roots and branches. If you use them well, you don't need magic words."

Questions about
Two Sisters

1. How was the land that Ella inherited different from the property Gretta had?

   _____

   _____

2. What did Ella do to make her farm successful?

   _____

   _____

3. What did Gretta think Ella did to grow cartloads of fruit and vegetables?

   _____

4. Why did Gretta think she was growing more fruit after she took the second tree?

   _____

5. In what ways did Ella try to help her sister?

   _____

   _____

   _____

6. Explain this statement made by Ella: "Enchanting perhaps, dear sister, but not enchanted."

   _____

   _____

Two Sisters

Characterization

Ella and Gretta were the main characters in the story *Two Sisters*. Think about their behaviors and personalities. How were they alike? How were they different?

Write words and phrases in the Venn diagram to analyze the two characters.

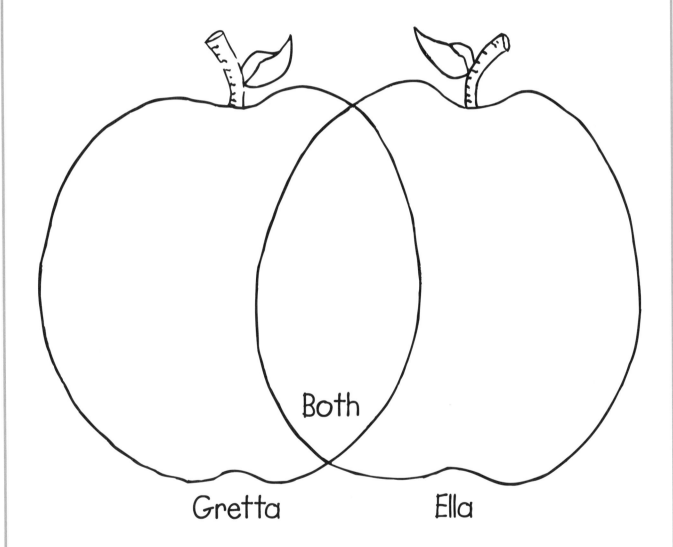

Both

Gretta   Ella

Name _____

Two Sisters

Vocabulary

A. Write each of these words from the story next to its definition.

inherited   prosperous   orchards   complain   misfortune
terracing   cultivating   prune   sturdy   worthless

1. _____ strong, not wobbly

2. _____ bad luck

3. _____ to tell why you think something is not right or is unfair

4. _____ a way to plant crops on hillsides to keep soil in place

5. _____ helping plants improve and grow

6. _____ to trim the branches

7. _____ without value

8. _____ fields of trees that produce fruit

9. _____ successful, doing well

10. _____ given the property of someone who has died

B. Many words in this story have to do with farming or growing plants. Write the words that go with each item below.

1. Six words that refer to plants or plant names:

_____   _____   _____

_____   _____   _____

2. Six words that refer to work farmers do:

_____   _____   _____

_____   _____   _____

3. Write a word from the story that means the same as "land."

_____

Name _____

Two Sisters

Homophones

Homophones are words that sound the same, but have different meanings.

1. Find the words in the story that are homophones for these words.

knot _____   sew _____   there _____

pair _____   dew _____   knight _____

deer _____   ewe _____   whole _____

heir _____   knead _____   rein _____

2. Fill in the blanks in these sentences with the correct homophone.

a. **hole   whole   for   four**

That package is _____ Abigail.

If you take the _____ pie, there won't be any left for Arnold.

There were _____ chairs near the desk.

There was a large _____ in my sweater.

b. **weight   wait   pair   pear**

I had a yellow _____ for lunch today.

I will _____ until Friday for a new supply of paper.

What is the _____ of four bags of apples?

He placed an extra _____ of socks in his backpack.

c. **there   their   sea   see**

If you look over _____, you will see the playground.

_____ pictures were placed on the bulletin board so everyone

could _____ them.

Waves from the _____ rolled up onto the beach.

Out of Space

Ten years had passed since we had blasted off Worim. All the planets in our star system were so crowded we couldn't find a place to land. I wanted to stay on Worim and do the best we could, but my folks wouldn't hear of it. "The worms have eaten everything that was green and most things that aren't," Mom said. "We could be next."

"It's now or never," Dad said. "Who would have thought that those cute little pet worms everyone had would have taken over the planet?"

"What if we don't find a new place?" I asked.

"We'll just take in the scenery," Dad answered. "Maybe we'll come to another star system that isn't plagued with worms."

I was so bored, I didn't even bother to watch the asteroids, moons, planets, or all the garbage whizzing by. There were all these broken down spaceships, satellites, and out-of-business fast-food places. People just threw them out when they were done with them instead of disposing of them in a black hole. It was so bad that the intergalactic TV programs we tried to watch came in garbled. I'd watched some great ones from a place called Earth. Most of the creatures on the programs were strange, but a few looked like us. Mom said I watched too much TV anyway. I don't know what she thinks I should do. We ran out of books to read and we haven't seen a library for five years. Our communication system isn't much better. Sometimes we hear strange signals. There was one about shooting baskets. I couldn't figure out why anyone would want to hurt a basket. I told Dad he'd better be careful where we went down. There could be something worse than worms on some of the planets.

Mom suggested I do something useful in the garden or the science lab. That worked for a year or two. We grew the same old food all the time so it got boring. I designed a robot in the lab that took care of the garden. Sometimes I took off my gravity suit and tried air swimming. I floated around and did all sorts of stunts. That got boring too. Every year or two, Dad anchored the transport to some space junk and we took a space walk.

 Read and Understand, Fiction • Grades 4–6 • EMC 748

Early this morning we hitched a ride on some light beams traveling from stars. The transport really sped along. Suddenly Dad steered the space transport off a beam. "Look at this!" he said. Mom and I peered through the monitor. It was another star system. We circled the first planet. It looked deserted. Dad set the anti-gravity button and turned on the search beams. We went in for a better look. It was too small and too cold. We traveled on without getting out to see what it was like. Mom traded places with Dad so he could have a turn at the monitor. Some of the planets were nothing but gas and noxious fumes. There wasn't anything to eat on any of them.

"Look out!" said Mom. "Take cover!" There were flying bits of matter everywhere. Mom was a great driver. She miniaturized our ship and we managed to get through the meteor storm.

When everything was back to normal, we resumed our regular size. By that time we were closer to the star. "Look! I think we're home," Dad said. We hadn't seen a planet like this since our own star system. There were clouds swirling over the planet, signs of water, green spaces, deserts, everything a Worim needs. Mom came in close and Dad turned on the testing equipment. "It's possible," he said, "but it seems heavily populated."

We circled the planet a few times, looking for a place to land. The cities had a lot of smoke around them. "No Worim could survive there," Dad said. Finally he pointed at the screen. "Right here!"

We floated down to a green world and parked the transport under the biggest plant I had ever seen.

"It's time to mingle," Mom said, "and see what creatures are here."

The strange beings we saw stared back at us. A few ran off. I asked one for directions to a library, but the creature ran away without speaking. "A little rude, I'd say." Dad shook his head and said, "They could use a little Worim etiquette."

We came to a huge building with the word *Museum* on the front of it. When we walked inside, we knew we'd have to leave the planet quickly. "Poor fellow! There must have been some gigantic worms here to do something like this," Dad said.

We stared at the skeleton of a giant *Maiasaura*. "It looks just like my Aunt Worima," said Mom, "only a lot bigger." We walked past several more skeletons and looked at the charts and murals on the walls. "Look at that!" I said. "There are others here just like us." The sign above the picture said *Psittacosaurus*.

"That's us," Dad agreed. We were feeling a little better until we saw creatures with nets moving toward us. "Get 'em!" one said. We pulled ourselves upright and almost flew out the door. We didn't stop running until we were inside the transport and on our way up.

Questions about *Out of Space*

1. What caused the Worims to leave their planet?

    _____

    _____

2. Why didn't they go to another planet in their star system?

    _____

3. What did the narrator believe space creatures should do with spaceships, satellites, and out-of-business fast-food places?

    _____

    _____

4. List four activities that the narrator found to do on the space transport.

    _____

    _____

    _____

5. How did you know that the narrator liked to read?

    _____

    _____

6. Where do you think the Worims landed? Explain your answer.

    _____

    _____

7. Why did the Worims leave the new planet?

    _____

    _____

Out of Space

Think about It

1. What clues in the story told you that the Worims are dinosaurlike creatures?

   _____

   _____

2. What could have happened to the Worims if they had stayed on the new planet? Write three possibilities.

   _____

   _____

   _____

3. Write a new ending to the story. Tell what happens when the Worims are captured by the creatures with the nets.

   _____

   _____

   _____

   _____

   _____

   _____

   _____

   _____

   _____

   _____

   _____

Out of Space

Vocabulary

Complete the sentences using these words from the story.

scenery	plagued	asteroid	disposing	garbled	deserted
communication	designed	anchored	transport	hitched	heavy populated
noxious	gigantic	mingle	etiquette	intergalactic	

1. The _____ fumes came from his laboratory.

2. They were _____ by problems with their _____

   system, and they couldn't receive messages that weren't _____.

3. He _____ a new robot that would do the work for him.

4. The city was _____ _____, and there wasn't
   enough housing for all the people.

5. They decided to _____ with the creatures there to see what they
   were like.

6. They _____ the space _____ and went outside
   to take a walk.

7. The _____ didn't change very much for long periods of time.

8. They traveled through an _____ belt when they were coming
   into the star system.

9. They were on an _____ mission to find a new planet and
   star system.

10. Rules for good _____ include speaking politely to others.

11. They _____ the wagon to the horse.

12. They could see no sign of life on the planet. It was _____.

13. The planet was inhabited by _____ worms.

14. They were letting their junk drift in space rather than _____ of
    it properly.

Name _____

Out of Space

Syllables

Write the number of syllables in each word below. Then find the words in the word search.

anchor _____   garbled _____   murals _____   satellite _____

communication _____   gigantic _____   museum _____   scenery _____

deserted _____   gravity _____   noxious _____   skeletons _____

designed _____   intergalactic _____   plagued _____   transport _____

etiquette _____   mingle _____   populated _____

```
A L D T R Z P S K N E P Z K O
C O M M U N I C A T I O N T L
P L A G U E D E G R A V I T Y
M E X I T Y L N T D P D D I P
U T L G S A T E L L I T E N O
R I N A N N O R D G X R S T P
A Q A N I C Y Y R A S A I E U
L U A T H H Z E W R S N G R L
S E T I L O T O O B Z S N G A
M T E C S R M N O L B P E A T
R T U S S P H E R E N O D L E
S E D E S E R T E D L R B A D
S O N G M I N G L E B T W C S
H A P P Y Z N O X I O U S T L
T M N S K E L E T O N S T I O
E A S Y K M U S E U M L A C D
```

The Gift

Great-Grandma had taken care of me when I was little, and now I had to help her. She had a small house next door to ours, and she could do some of the cleaning, but Mom and I did most of it. She ate dinner with us, and Mom drove her to appointments and took her shopping. Mom worked, so it was up to me to help G-G-Ma (that's what I call her) after school. Sometimes I wanted to go places with my friends or watch TV, but then I remembered that G-G-Ma used to give up time with her friends so she could take care of me. I like talking to G-G-Ma too. She's told me what life was like when she was growing up and some funny stories about Mom. The best part is she always has time to listen to me, laugh at a joke, or give me a hug when I need one. She throws in extra hugs even when nothing goes wrong.

Today is a special day. We've planned a surprise for G-G-Ma's ninety-first birthday. Last night we baked the cake. When Mom gets home from work, she'll cook G-G-Ma's favorite dinner. I wanted to find a perfect gift, but I couldn't think of anything. I made her a card and I wrote a poem to go with it. Mom said that was enough, but I wanted to find something special—something that would make her happy. I went shopping with Mom last Saturday, but nothing seemed quite right. G-G-Ma didn't need another sweater or an apron. She has enough towels and clothes to last another ninety-one years. Her house has lots of knickknacks and figurines. I know she doesn't want more, because they are hard to dust. We came home without finding anything.

I unlocked the door and called out. "I'm home from school." There wasn't any answer. I went into the kitchen. There was G-G-Ma sitting on a kitchen chair watching a tiny orange kitten eat little scraps of leftover chicken.

"She was lost and hungry," G-G-Ma said. "I heard her crying outside. Probably somebody just dumped her." The kitten finished the food and scratched around.

"I'll take her out," I said. I picked up the kitten and put her outside.

 Read and Understand, Fiction • Grades 4–6 • EMC 748

"It's better to leave her there," G-G-Ma said, looking worried. "I can't take care of a kitten–an old lady like me. I can't always take care of myself. Maybe she'll find a home. She's a lot like my Belle—the same color."

I remembered how much G-G-Ma had loved Belle. That cat had followed her everywhere. She played with the broom when G-G-Ma swept the floor, she rolled spools of thread all over the house, and she slept at the foot of G-G-Ma's bed. Sometimes G-G-Ma talks about Belle like she's still here.

We heard the kitten meowing and scratching at the door. G-G-Ma got up and walked to the door. She put her hand on the doorknob. "It's hard to turn anything away when it needs your help," she said. "But I can't take care of a kitten."

I put my arm around G-G-Ma. "I'll find a home for it," I said. I let the kitten in. When G-G-Ma sat in the chair again, I put the kitten in her lap. It batted at G-G-Ma's fingers and then curled up. She petted the kitten and laughed.

"I'd forgotten how soft a kitten is."

I have a big dog that has too much energy. I have to keep the dog away from G-G-Ma so he doesn't knock her down. I couldn't keep a kitten too. Mom said "one pet," and I knew she meant it. Most of my friends had pets already, but I had to do something.

"I'll be back in a few minutes," I said, and I went over to my house. I called Mom and told her about the kitten and my plan. At first she didn't like it, but I kept talking and finally she agreed.

Mom knocked on G-G-Ma's door at about 5:30. I let her in. I'd helped G-G-Ma tie a button on a string. She sat in the chair and played with the kitten.

Mom put down a bunch of sacks and hugged G-G-Ma. "Happy birthday!"

"I'd forgotten all about it," G-G-Ma said. "Look at this kitten, Martha. Sally helped me make this toy. You know my fingers aren't too good at putting things together anymore. I know I can't keep the kitten, but it sure has brightened my day. Sally says she'll find a home for it."

"She already has," Mom said. She put a bag of cat food on the kitchen counter. "You can open the bag and feed the kitten the dry food when she needs it. Sally will feed it the canned food every day. I have litter, a box, bowls for food and water, and some toys. It's your birthday present. We'll all take care of the kitten, but you'll have to help too. It will give you something to do during the day."

G-G-Ma started to cry, but I knew it wasn't because she was sad. I gave her a tissue. Then I took out all the cat supplies Mom had brought home.

"We'll bring dinner over here tonight. Get ready to celebrate," Mom said. "Sally can come help me carry everything when she gets the kitten set up. Tomorrow we'll make an appointment for a kitten checkup." Mom picked up the kitten. "I've missed Belle too," she said.

Name _____

Questions about *The Gift*

1. What did Sally, the narrator in the story, like about helping her great-grandmother?

2. What did Sally and her mother plan for G-G-Ma's birthday?

3. Why couldn't Sally find a special gift for G-G-Ma?

4. Even though she liked the kitten, G-G-Ma said they should leave it outside. Why do you think she said that?

5. Why couldn't Sally keep the kitten?

6. What did Sally do to see that G-G-Ma got a special birthday gift? How did Sally's mother contribute to the gift?

Name _____

The Gift

Compound Words

There are several compound words in the story. Find the words and write them next to their definitions.

a. _____ a part of a door

b. _____ all around

c. _____ saved for another meal

d. _____ all things

e. _____ figurines and objects

f. _____ any object

g. _____ your parent's grandmother

h. _____ an age

i. _____ the opposite of inside

j. _____ part of the time

k. _____ the anniversary of the day you were born

■ ■

To and Too

Choose the correct homophone for each sentence.

to   too

a. They had _____ many books for the bookcase.

b. They were going _____ Mary's house.

c. He gave the book _____ Tom.

d. Armando would like to have extra paper _____.

e. She would like _____ skate home.

The Gift

Contractions

Contractions are two words that are put together and shortened. The letters that are taken from the words are replaced with an apostrophe. For example, the word *couldn't* means *could not*. The *o* is replaced by the **apostrophe**.

A. The following contractions are found in the story. Write the two words that mean the same as each contraction.

1. She's _____

2. didn't _____

3. I'll _____

4. can't _____

5. she'll _____

6. I'd _____

7. we'll _____

8. you'll _____

9. I've _____

B. The word *it's* is a contraction for *it is*. The word *its* without the apostrophe is possessive and **shows ownership**. Write *it's* or *its* in these sentences.

1. _____ Saturday and we are going to the park.

2. Put _____ food on the counter.

3. _____ not the movie I want to see.

4. I think _____ the best choice.

5. _____ color is the same as the other cat's.

C. Write a sentence for each of these two words: its, it's

_____

_____

Name _____

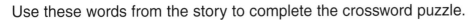

The Gift
Crossword Puzzle

Use these words from the story to complete the crossword puzzle.

Word Box					
brightened	thread	kitten	remembered	special	figurines
energy	supplies	spools	forgotten	appointments	

Across
3. scheduled times to be places
6. needed items
7. a young cat
8. physical vigor, effort
9. a slender string used for sewing
10. perked up

Down
1. recalled
2. small glass animals and people
4. having significant meaning
5. not remembered
6. they hold thread

The Tower

King Alexander wanted the moon. He was sure the moon was filled with gold. He had a rule that all gold should belong to the greatest king in the universe. Since he had passed a rule that he was the greatest king in the universe, he felt entitled to that gold. "I must add the moon to the royal treasury," he said.

"Impossible," said the royal advisor. "It's beyond your reach. If your royal hands can't touch it, neither can anyone else. The moon is safe where it is."

The king watched the moon shrink and grow. "Someone must be able to reach the moon," the king reasoned. He set his telescope on the thin crescent moon. "Not only has someone reached it, he's been stealing my gold. It's almost gone. If I can catch the thief, the moon will always grow bigger and it will never shrink." Of course the king did not stop to think that if a thief were taking the gold out of the moon, the same thief, or someone else, was filling it up again.

"Bring me the wisest person in the kingdom. I need help if I am to reach the moon," the king demanded of his advisor.

"But, your highness, you proclaimed yourself the wisest person in the kingdom."

"Then bring me the second-wisest person in the kingdom."

The royal advisor searched the kingdom. All the king's subjects knew about the king's royal temper. If they did not do what he asked, he would toss them into the royal jail. No one would assume the role of the second-wisest person.

The royal advisor continued his search. One day he saw two goatherds caring for their animals on the slopes of a mountain.

"Good day," called the royal advisor. "I am looking for the second-wisest person in the kingdom."

"That must be my older brother," said one of the goatherds, pointing to the second goatherd. "He knows where to find the best grasses and plants in the land. Our goats provide rich milk that is made into the finest cheese in the kingdom."

"Wise indeed," said the royal advisor. "If you come with me, you can help our king with a difficult problem."

"Indeed, I will," said the goatherd. "I know everything there is to know about goats."

The goatherd and the royal advisor arrived at the palace and went to the king. "Your highness," the royal advisor said, "this goatherd is the second-wisest person in the kingdom. He will help you reach the moon."

"The moon?" asked the goatherd. "I thought you needed help with goats."

"What would I do with goats?" the king asked. "Since you are the second-wisest person in the kingdom, you must find a way to reach the moon. You have seven days to come up with a plan. If you don't think of something, I will throw you and the royal advisor in jail forever."

The royal advisor took the confused goatherd to his room. They drew and talked half the night trying to think of a plan. Finally they could stay awake no longer. While the goatherd slept, he dreamed he was back with his goats. He dreamed about the fresh apples in the trees. He stood on an old barrel to reach the fruit high up in the tree.

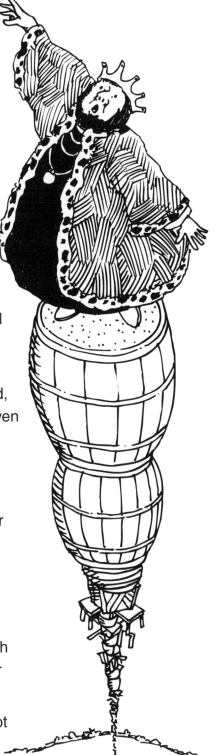

The next morning he called for the advisor and told him about the dream. They drew a picture of a great tower and marched off to see the king.

"Your highness, we have the answer," said the royal advisor. "Have the royal tax collector bring every barrel in the kingdom. We'll have the royal carpenter fasten them together into a tower. You can climb to the top and reach the moon."

The whole kingdom watched the tower grow from the ground, past the trees, higher than the castle walls. Every piece of wood, even beds and chairs, were added to the tower.

"It's high enough," King Alexander said one day. "I'll wait no longer. Today is the day I'll climb to the moon."

"Your highness," said the advisor, "you could send me in your place. It's a very long climb."

"Since I am the greatest king in the universe and the wisest person in the kingdom," the king answered, "I will have the honor of reaching the moon first. You may climb up later with my dinner."

When the king reached the very top, he stretched up to touch the moon. "I must be a little higher," he called out. "Send up another chair or box—anything."

"I fear there is nothing left," the royal advisor called back. "Not even a butter churn."

"Then take something off the bottom and throw it up here," the king answered.

"Your majesty," the goatherd said, "that's impossible. If we take one off the bottom, the tower…"

"I command you to take something off the bottom!" the king bellowed.

The goatherd looked at the royal advisor. The royal advisor nodded, and the goatherd pulled a barrel from the bottom of the tower.

Name _____

Questions about *The Tower*

1. How did the king's rules ensure that he would get the gold in the moon?

   _____

   _____

2. In what ways did the king show his stupidity?

   _____

   _____

   _____

3. Why did the royal advisor bring the goatherd to the king?

   _____

   _____

4. Why did the royal advisor decide to help the goatherd?

   _____

   _____

5. What was the inspiration for the goatherd's plan?

   _____

   _____

6. Do you think the goatherd was clever or stupid? Give a fact or facts to support your opinion.

   _____

   _____

7. Write a final sentence for the story.

   _____

   _____

The Tower

Vocabulary

A. Write each word below on the line next to its meaning.

universe	entitled	treasury	impossible	beyond	royal
telescope	crescent	proclaimed	provide	carpenter	command

1. _____ to give what is needed

2. _____ can't be done

3. _____ all galaxies and solar systems

4. _____ a person who makes things from wood

5. _____ an order

6. _____ announced with authority

7. _____ deserves to have

8. _____ where money and valuable objects are stored

9. _____ an object that enables someone to see distant objects more clearly

10. _____ a shape of the moon

11. _____ having to do with kings, queens, and their families

12. _____ farther away

B. Write two terms in the story that are used to address the king.

_____   _____

Name _____

The Tower

Problems and Solutions

Most characters in stories have problems that they try to solve throughout the story. Write the following statements about the story under the correct headings.

had to come up with a plan	needed help to reach the moon
came across two goatherds	might get thrown into jail too
thought gold was being stolen	still couldn't reach the moon
sent his advisor to find the second-wisest person	helped the goatherd
had to find the second-wisest person	demanded that something be taken off the bottom
dreamed about picking fruit	
decided to catch the thief	

Royal Advisor

Problems   Solutions

_____   _____

_____   _____

_____   _____

Goatherd

Problems   Solutions

_____   _____

_____   _____

_____   _____

King Alexander

Problems   Solutions

_____   _____

_____   _____

_____   _____

The Tower

Point of View

In *The Tower* a storyteller is relating the events. Imagine the story from the goatherd's viewpoint. How would the story change?

Write a retelling of *The Tower* from this new viewpoint.

_____

_____

_____

_____

_____

_____

_____

_____

_____

_____

_____

_____

_____

_____

_____

_____

The Missing Ring

Anna slipped her mother's ring onto her finger. She watched the gems sparkle in the sunlight that streamed through the open window.

"Anna, please hurry with the thread," her mother called. "I need more blue for the forget-me-nots."

Anna set the ring back on the dresser and hurried downstairs. "Here," she said, admiring the blouse her mother was embroidering. "I'm sure it will win a prize at the fair."

"Win or lose," her mother said, "it's a family tradition. Your great-grandmother entered her first quilt 50 years ago. Now, with machines to do the work, it seems foolish to do all this by hand. At the same time, while I work I remember your grandmother, my mother, and all of us talking and sewing. I still hear my mother say, 'Mary, that stitch is not straight.' I fretted at the time when I had to pull it out, but now it makes me smile to think about it. I guess I'll never lose the sewing habit."

"It's almost four, you'd better be on your way to soccer practice. I understand there's a big game this Saturday."

Anna laughed. She'd be playing against Sally, her cousin and best friend. "I guess you'll have to yell for both teams, Mom."

"I'll be there with my loudest cheer," Mom called as Anna hurried out the door.

When Anna returned home, her mother met her at the door. "Did you take my ring?" she asked. "I set it on the dresser so it wouldn't catch on the threads. It's not there."

"I did put it on my finger, but I didn't take it. I put it back on the dresser where I found it." The ring was another tradition. It had been in the family for a hundred years, maybe longer.

"Anna, are you sure? I won't be angry. It couldn't fly away."

"I didn't take it. Really I didn't. I'll help you look for it, though." Anna hurried upstairs. She searched the floor around the dresser and under the bed. She checked every corner of the room. The ring was gone. Did her mother really think she had lost it? Anna closed the bedroom window and hurried downstairs to help with dinner.

"It was there," she said, "on the dresser when I brought the thread down. I looked everywhere. I didn't take it."

At dinner that night, Anna's mother told her dad about the ring. "You don't suppose someone could have stolen it? Anna says she didn't take it."

"Not too likely," her dad said. Anna's parents looked at her suspiciously.

Somehow, Anna had to find that ring. She searched the house that week whenever she had time. She found lost socks, books, and a yo-yo missing since last summer, but no ring.

The morning before the soccer game, Anna looked in her mom's dresser drawer for bands to pull her hair back from her face. There on the window ledge was a sleek-feathered crow.

The bird watched her, then hopped to the floor and picked up a silver bead from her mother's sewing basket. The crow flew out the window and into a nest in the tree. Anna hurried down the stairs and ran to the door.

"Anna, wait. We'll go to the game together," her mother said.

"I'm not going to the game yet. Please, Mom, help me with the ladder. I can't do this by myself," Anna called. "I think I know where your ring is."

"Anna, be serious. I am very upset about losing the ring, but this is ridiculous. You've looked for it all week." Anna's mother ran after her and helped her with the extension ladder. "What are you doing?" she asked as they carried the ladder to the big pine tree in the center of the lawn.

"I'm going to catch a thief," Anna said. "Don't worry. Just help me set the ladder against the tree and hold on so it doesn't fall with me on it."

She started up the ladder. "Be careful!" her mother called.

Anna's knees were shaking by the time she was halfway up the ladder. She'd climbed ladders before to pick fruit, but this was different. The crow's nest was a lot higher than she thought. Just don't look down, she said to herself.

Her mother was calling, "Anna, don't climb any higher. Come down."

Anna couldn't answer. Climbing down might be worse than going up. She didn't have to go any higher, anyway. She could see in the nest. The crow had flown off. There were buttons, beads, and a pile of bright, shiny objects. Anna sorted through the crow's stolen treasures. There it was—the ring. She put it on her finger. Slowly and carefully she climbed down the ladder. At least the crow wasn't there to dive at her.

When Anna touched the ground, she handed the ring to her mother. "You were wrong about it flying away. It flew off in a crow's beak. I caught the thief taking a bead from your sewing basket."

"It's time to put a screen on that window." Anna's mother hugged her and put the ring back on Anna's finger. "You can wear it for good luck until the game."

Questions about *The Missing Ring*

1. What two traditions were important in Anna's family?

2. Were Anna's parents wrong to think she had lost the ring? Why or why not?

3. How do you know that Anna felt bad about the missing ring?

4. How did Anna discover what had happened to the ring?

5. What clue in the beginning of the story helps to explain the missing ring?

6. Tell about how Anna retrieved the missing ring. Include how she felt during this experience.

7. Why did Mother give Anna the ring to wear for a while?

Name _____

The Missing Ring
Vocabulary

A. Use these words to fill in the blanks in the sentences.

admiring	embroidering	tradition	fretted
serious	ridiculous	extension	suspiciously

1. Entering the sewing contest at the fair was a family _____.

2. Anna's mother was _____ a blouse.

3. The ring was beautiful and Anna was _____ it.

4. The _____ ladder could reach high places.

5. The clown's act was _____.

6. Her mother _____ about making sewing mistakes when she was young.

7. Her parents thought she had lost the ring and they looked at her

   _____.

8. Having the ring disappear was very _____.

B. A **root** or **base** word is the basic word to which prefixes and suffixes may be added. For example, the root (base) word of *ridiculous* is *ridicule*.

Write the root word and the suffix of the words below.

	root word	suffix
admiring	_____	_____
embroidering	_____	_____
fretted	_____	_____
suspiciously	_____	_____
extension	_____	_____

Name _____

The Missing Ring
Sequencing

Number these events in the order in which they happened in the story.

_____ She found the ring.

_____ Anna climbed the ladder to the crow's nest.

_____ When Anna came home from soccer practice the ring was missing.

_____ Anna tried on the ring.

_____ Anna went to soccer practice.

_____ Anna looked for the ring.

_____ Anna saw the crow take the bead from the sewing basket and fly off.

_____ She put the ring on the dresser.

Circle the words below in the word search.

```
T R I D I C U L O U S S
R E M B R O I D E R S E
A S U S P I C I O U S R
D L E D G E N A R A F I
I S T I T C H D R L R O
T L M B G E M M D A E U
I E X T E N S I O N T S
O E E N M S C R O W O M
N K B L S O D E L M U T
```

Word Box						
suspicious	ridiculous	ledge	sleek	tradition	gems	admire
fret	embroider	extension	crow	stitch	serious	

128 Read and Understand, Fiction • Grades 4–6 • EMC 748

Name _____

The Missing Ring

Writing about Personal Experiences

A **tradition** is a belief or a custom that is handed down from one generation to another. Several traditions were important in the story *The Missing Ring.* Think of a tradition that is important to your family, school, or community. Describe the tradition, then use it as the basis for an original story.

_____

_____

_____

_____

_____

_____

_____

_____

_____

_____

_____

_____

_____

_____

_____

_____

_____

_____

_____

_____

_____

_____

Play Ball!

Eduardo walked his bike along the gravel path that led to the farm. No use wearing out the tires. They had to last another month until the end of school. Besides, he was tired. It was a three-mile ride from school to the farm where his parents worked. He was lucky to have the bike. He had earned enough money weeding and hoeing during spring vacation to buy it. The Martinez family needed some money for their trip back to Texas, so he had bought Manuel's bike. Since he didn't have to take the school bus home anymore, he tried out for the baseball team. Practice was after school. He was in the outfield and hitting better every practice. He'd have to work during the summer to earn money for school next fall, but his dad said he could play baseball for now.

Eduardo had been at the same school for three months. His family never stayed anywhere very long. Now he was catching up on reading and math. Science was the best. Eduardo didn't like going to so many schools. He had to make new friends and he was always behind with the work. Dad had promised they'd stay here until summer if they could. He said he wanted Eduardo and his brothers to learn something, so they could have any job they wanted someday.

Every evening Eduardo helped his two younger brothers with their homework. His parents were too tired after working in the fields all day. They had to be back at work by 5:00 A.M. It was up to Eduardo to get his brothers ready for bed and off to school.

Eduardo stopped before he reached his house. His dad was outside, loading up the van with everything from the house. His mom and some of the neighbors helped.

Eduardo ran to the van. "Why?" he yelled at his dad. "You said we'd stay until school was out. We can't go now. The first baseball game is this Saturday!"

"I didn't have time to come tell you," his dad said. "*Hijo,* I'm sorry. Your Uncle Alberto sent this letter. If we get to the Williams's ranch in the valley tomorrow, we'll have work all summer. They'll hold the job until then. We'll have to travel overnight. There's a better place to live there and more money."

Eduardo hit the van with his fist. "There's one more month before school is out. We can wait. There'll be a job somewhere."

"Hey, calm down, *hijo!* It'll be better there. There will be more family. Maybe if this job is good enough we'll have enough for our own farm. Then you won't have to change schools anymore. Maybe you can play baseball all the time."

"Look! I've got space on top for the *bicicleta.* Come on. Let's get it up there."

Eduardo helped his dad lift the bike. He held it down while his dad tied it to the folding chairs and other furniture on top. When they finished, his dad hugged him.

I didn't get to say good-bye to everyone, Eduardo thought. They'll wonder why I didn't show up for practice. And his teacher, the books in his backpack—how would he take care of that?

"Dad, the books for homework—how do we get them back to school?"

"Ask Roberto. He goes to the same school. He can take them tomorrow."

Roberto was only in third grade, but he'd do it. He wouldn't throw the books away somewhere like some kids would.

Eduardo collected his books and those his brothers had. He walked to Roberto's house, talked to Roberto's parents, and gave them the books. He took a paper from his notebook. "I'm going to write a letter to my teacher," he explained.

"You're always a good boy," Roberto's mother said. "I keep telling Roberto that. He should be like you."

Eduardo laughed and gave Roberto a high five. "He's the best there is. Don't worry about Roberto." Eduardo sat at the table and began to write.

Dear Miss Simms,

I'm glad you taught me how to write a letter today. My family had to leave for the valley. My dad got a good job at the Williams's ranch, like a foreman or something, maybe. Please say good-bye to my friends and the baseball team. I hope they win every game.

Eduardo

It wasn't really true about the foreman's job, but it sounded like a good reason. Somehow it felt better letting everyone know what had happened. He didn't want anyone to think he didn't like the team or school.

As the van rolled down the gravel road, his dad turned up the radio and started singing. He always sang off-key, and it made everybody laugh. His mom passed food around. Next spring there'd be baseball somewhere. With a little more money he could buy a ball and a bat. His brothers were getting bigger. Maybe they could all play on Sundays in a field or somewhere. Maybe he'd decide to play in the big leagues someday. The "maybe's" again. He was sounding just like his dad.

Questions about *Play Ball!*

1. How did Eduardo get a bicycle?

   _____

   _____

2. What did the bicycle represent in Eduardo's life?

   _____

   _____

3. Why did Eduardo's family move so often?

   _____

   _____

4. How did Eduardo feel when he got home that day? Why?

   _____

   _____

5. Eduardo could be described as "conscientious." List at least two facts from the story that support that statement.

   _____

   _____

   _____

6. To be "optimistic" means to expect or hope for the best. How was Eduardo optimistic at the end of the story?

   _____

   _____

   _____

Bonus: Do you know why there is an exclamation mark after "Play Ball" in the title?

   _____

Name _____

Play Ball!
Vocabulary

1. Match the two Spanish words that are in the story to the English words below. Use clues in the story to help you.

    a. bicycle _____   b. son _____

2. Use these words to complete the sentences.

    travel   collected   neighbors   practice   science
    foreman   homework   promised   maybe   gravel

    a. There was a _____ road that led to the farm.

    b. The _____ helped load the van.

    c. Eduardo liked studying _____.

    d. Eduardo _____ his brother's books.

    e. Eduardo helped his brothers with their _____.

    f. Eduardo's family had to _____ overnight.

    g. His dad _____ they'd stay until school was out.

    h. Baseball _____ was after school.

    i. Eduardo said his dad had a job as a _____.

    j. His dad was always saying "_____."

3. Write sentences using each of these words:

    travel   collected   promised   practice

    _____

    _____

    _____

    _____

Name _____

Play Ball!
Compound Words

A. A **compound word** is made up of two words. Find the compound words in the story that go with each item below.

1. two compound words that begin with *any*

   _____   _____

2. three compound words that begin with *every*

   _____   _____   _____

3. two compound words that end with *where*

   _____   _____

4. two compound words that begin with *some*

   _____   _____

5. the compound word that is the opposite of *inside*

   _____

6. the compound word that means *during the night*

   _____

7. the compound word that is a sport

   _____

8. the compound word for something that can be written in

   _____

9. the compound word that names lessons done after school

   _____

10. the compound word for something you could use to carry books

    _____

11. the compound word is a place on the baseball field

    _____

B. Choose two of the compound words from the story and write a sentence for each one on the back of this paper.

Play Ball!

A Character Map

Complete this character map to show what kind of a person Eduardo is. Write a descriptive heading in each of the empty boxes. Write one or more facts from the story that support each heading.

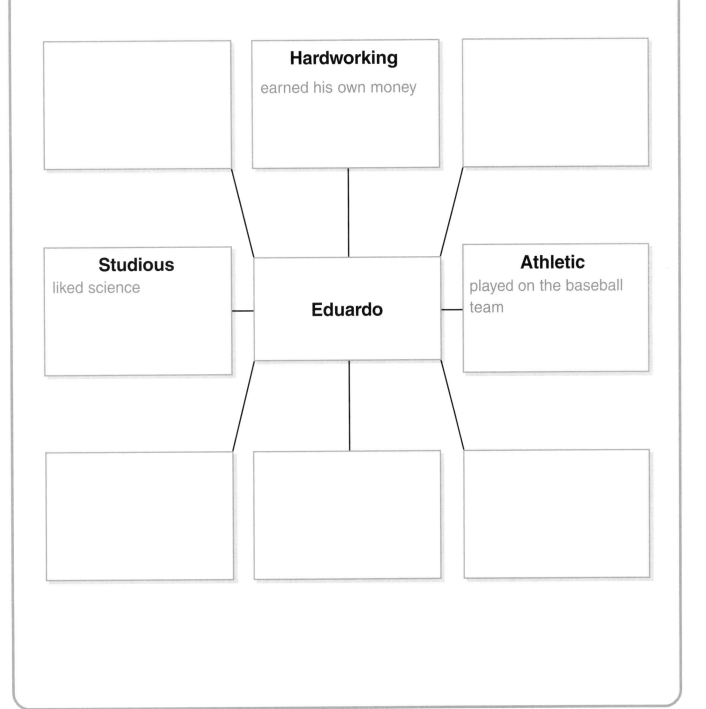

Hardworking

earned his own money

Studious

liked science

Eduardo

Athletic

played on the baseball team

Answer Key

Page 6
1. She knitted Stormalong a hammock that stretched from New Bedford, MA, to Newport, RI.
2. He had outgrown all the other boats. His boat would be the biggest ship that ever sailed the ocean.
3. He named the boat *Colossus* because that means "gigantic, enormous."
4. It ran into the tip of South America and broke it into pieces.
5. Throughout his life he was always helpful and considerate of the welfare of "normal" people.
6. Answers will vary. The information should include the storm, rescuing boats and seamen, the storm lets up, and Stormalong's trip to the sky.

Page 7
1. starboard, port
2. hammock
3. steeple
4. halibut
5. strait
6. latter
7. christened
8. former
9. anchored

1. unfurled
2. raged, tremendous
3. immense
4. exquisite

Page 8
4 saw
8 first
5 tied
6 hired
3 enormous
9 welcomed
2 hurried
7 last
1 named

1. rushed, greeted
2. christened
3. immense
4. watched
5. signed on
6. fastened
7. latter, former

Page 9
Stormalong was a big baby: he outgrew his cradle in a week; he had to sleep in the barn because the house was too small; at two he was taller than the church steeple; his hammock stretched from one state to another

Stormalong earned money to build his ship: when he carried fish from ships to the shore

Stormalong didn't need a crew: he could do everything a hundred seamen could do and faster

Stormalong rescued ships and sailors from a Caribbean hurricane: he swam through towering waves; he piled up boats on the deck of the *Colossus;* he swam to land with the anchor in his teeth

Page 12
1. The iguana was too big to take care of or they didn't want him anymore.
2. a. garden
   b. apartments
   c. laundry room
   d. parking lot
   e. garbage cans
3. Iguanas like warm places.
4. The iguana was asleep.
5. Answers will vary. Information should include: She was friendly and invited the boys in. Everyone called her "aunt." She helped her sister. She drove Martin to her sister's house to look for Iggie.

Page 13
A. 1. pavement
    2. mealworms
    3. munched
    4. searched
    5. received
    6. scaly
    7. maintenance
    8. spiny
    9. batteries
    10. iguana
B. Any 10 of these words:
    outside, in, under, on, behind, inside, around, over, up, here, into, there, out, down, across, toward

Page 14
1. Answers will vary.
2. Answers will vary. The answer should include three of these words:
   something, outside, anymore, inside, everyone, anyone's, mealworms, everywhere, afternoon
3. bluebird, houseboat, firewood, sidewalk, streetcar, barefoot, breadsticks, outdated, overdue, sometime

Page 15
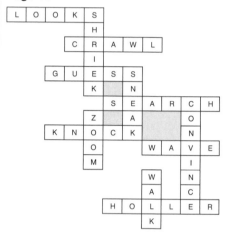

Page 18
1. She was afraid of the bear that lived in the forest. She felt fear.
2. He had never felt fear before and he wanted to know what it was.
3. a. the giant b. riding a flying tree in the sky c. falling into the water d. being underground in the cave with the bear
4. He would have to sit and listen to everyone's arguments and try to make everyone happy.
5. He could never do what he wanted to do again. Listening to people argue for 100 years and trying to make everyone happy was an impossible task.

Page 19
A. 1. filled
   2. wrong
   3. hot
   4. day
   5. fresh
B. 1. went, came
   2. here, there
   3. sky, earth
   4. under, over
   5. ran, walked
   6. started, stopped

   Read and Understand, Fiction • Grades 4–6 • EMC 748

7. new, old
8. in, out

Page 20
1. a. anger
   b. envy
   c. happiness
2. Answers will vary.
3. a. laurel wreath
   b. tremendous
   c. towering
   d. allergic
   e. peered

Page 21
1. in a village in the kingdom of Near and Far
2. forest, berry patch, sea, cave, village, town square
3. summer or fall
4. Berries were ripe.

Page 24
1. Answers will vary. The answer should include: He stampeded the cattle with coyote howls. Cowpunchers along the trail kept the cattle moving in the right direction.
2. He was raised by coyotes and thought he was one when he was a boy.
3. He could smell it and hear it.
4. He roped it and jumped on it.
5. The twister wasn't used to losing and became angry.
6. He threw them out of the twister and made a town for people moving west.
7. It wore itself out and turned into a gentle breeze.

Page 25
A. 1. bunkhouse
   2. stretch
   3. spooked
   4. gripped
   5. stationed
   6. cellar
   7. twister
   8. ballerina
   9. bareback
   10. fringe
   11. stampeded
B. The order may vary:
   1. cowpuncher
   2. wrangler
   3. cowpoke
   4. cowhand

Page 26
1. as truthful as a Sunday school teacher
2. as tall as a two-story house
3. like the points on a picket fence
4. so fringed it looked like blades of brown prairie grass
5. as calm as a hibernating bear
6. kicked up its tail like a bronco at a rodeo
7. as tired as a mother hen that had spent the day chasing after her chicks
8. as gentle as a newborn lamb frolicking across a meadow
9. like an angry panther chasing its dinner

Page 27
Answers will vary, but may include the following: No one is that tall; Coyotes don't raise children; You can't tell a twister what to do or show it where to go; A twister doesn't think about what it is doing or play games; You can't rope a mass of moving air and water; He couldn't put his spurs into air and water; He would be injured if he were caught in a twister; He could smell things 100 miles away; He dug a tunnel using his pet snake as a drill; He created a town out of the things picked up by the tornado.

Page 30
1. The previous owners had liked mice and thought they were useful. The new people were selfish, despised mice, and kept a cat.
2. ask the farmer's wife to put their food by their door; move
3. The farmer's wife did not like the mice. They couldn't get away with their possessions and children without being caught by the cat. They might end up in a place that was even more dangerous.
4. The cat interrupted their first meeting.
5. put a bell on the cat so the mice could hear it coming
6. None of them were brave enough to volunteer to bell the cat.
7. Answers will vary.

Page 31
1. volunteer
2. devour
3. encounters
4. possessions
5. uncontrollably

6. despise
7. solution
8. sensibly
9. cruel
10. replied
11. inner
12. selfish
13. fond
14. feline
15. doze
B. Answers will vary.

Page 32
1. a. fanged
   b. fiendish
   c. cruel
   d. furry
   e. horrifying
   f. prowls
   g. dangerous, lurks
   h. Disgusting
2. a. wonderful
   b. clever
3. The mice hate and fear the cat because it will kill them. The farmer's wife likes the cat because she regards the mice as pests; the cat is her pet.
4. hardworking, honest
5. selfish, despise mice, can't stand the sight of us
6. terrible

Page 33
1. "Leah…out," "Who…dilemma?"
2. "What..table?" "When…loop."
3. "Do…table?" "There…mousepower."
4. "What…idea!" "Let's…collar."

Page 36
1. The farmer hadn't watered or cared for him.
2. The dog said the farmer was lazy.
3. Hang it back on the tree.
4. The fisherman heard his basket talk, the weaver heard his cloth talk, and the swimmer heard the river talk. They were afraid.
5. Because yams, dogs, vines, rocks, baskets, cloth, and rivers can't talk.
6. Answers will vary.
7. The yam might not have said anything and the farmer wouldn't have met all the talking objects.

Page 37
1. a. alone
   b. unusual
   c. asked
   d. tangled
   e. stool
2. a. explained
   b. vine
   c. hare
   d. yam
   e. bundled
   f. weaver
   g. twisted
3. Answers will vary

Page 38
Personification
1. yam
2. dog
3. vine
4. rock
5. basket
6. cloth
7. river
8. golden stool
Setting
The garden: yam, dog, vine, rock
Along the path: basket, cloth, river
In the village: golden stool

Page 39
Compositions will vary.

Page 42
1. No one pleased both Ixtli and her father, the emperor.
2. He wanted to be near Ixtli to find out what kind of a person she was.
3. She was as kind as she was beautiful.
4. He came from a poor kingdom and he wanted to gather treasures to give to the emperor.
5. The emperor called Popo the "prince of nothing" and said he was not worthy to rule the kingdom.
6. She died of sadness when she thought he would never return.
7. Ixtli became the mountain, The Sleeping Woman, and Popo became a volcano watching over her.

Page 43
1. obsidian
2. ancient
3. bouquets
4. litter
5. quetzal
6. disguised
Emperor: angry, rich, powerful

Princess Ixtli: beautiful, kind, gentle, caring, despondent, grieving
Prince Popo: brave, strong, loyal, worthy

Page 44
1. Her eyes were a soft brown like the eyes of the deer...
2. Answers will vary.
3. Answers will vary.

Page 45

Page 48
1. He wanted something special to eat.
2. He tasted them until he found the perfect flavor.
3. He wanted to show off the cheese to the other crows and eat it in front of them.
4. He held the same opinions of himself—that he was better than other animals, he was more clever, and he could sing well.
5. flatter
6. boastful, a braggart
7. Beware of those who praise you when they have something to gain.

Page 49
1. a. iridescent
   b. jewels
   c. glistened
   d. rainbow
   e. clever
2. Answers should include at least six of these words:
   song, melodious, notes, music, serenade, concert, trilling, lullaby, musical
3. e, j, g, i, a, b, c, f, d, h, k

Page 50
1. No answer is required.
2. to see or know what will happen in the future
3. to make rich
4. to be filled with happiness or joy
5. not appealing
6. to plan or set up ahead of time
7. not able
8. to put back again
9. to give back
10. to alert to danger before it happens
11. vanish, not to appear or be seen
12. to form an incorrect opinion
13. to think differently; argue
14. bad luck

Page 51
Writings will vary.

Page 54
1. So she could go places wih her friends in the summer.
2. She ran errands and took care of pets.
3. She needed a walker to get around.
4. A person who volunteers does something to be helpful and doesn't expect pay, while a person who has a job for money expects to be paid.
5. She really wanted to use the money to get the bicycle. She was torn between what she wanted and what she knew was the correct action.
6. Answers will vary.
7. If you are responsible and honest, you will be rewarded.

Page 55
A. 1. repair
   2. uninteresting
   3. guests
   4. discovered
   5. relied
   6. money
   7. considerate
   8. separate
B. Mrs. Perry: dependable, thoughtful
   Alice: people really trust you

Page 56
A. 1. dependable
   2. quickly
   3. handful
   4. encouragement
   5. careless
   6. farmer
   7. finalist
   8. lighten
   9. happiness

B. 1. saying, circle "ing"; happiness, circle "ness"; helping, circle "ing"
   2. walked, circle "ed"; quickly, circle "ly"
   3. nameless, circle "less"
   4. helpful, circle "ful"
   5. pharmacist, circle "ist"; wheeled, circle "ed"

Page 57

Answers will vary. Possible answers:
   3. Margaret looked for the money and couldn't find it.
   4. She went home to decide what to do.
   5. She paid for the groceries with the money she had saved for her bicycle.

Page 60

   1. He crawled under chairs and tables to find lost objects.
      He brought in grass that could be woven into mats or shoes.
      He helped his father look for fallen branches.
   2. Answers will vary.
   3. The boat was a small bowl; the oars were pieces of chopsticks. He had a sewing needle for a sword and a piece of straw for a scabbard.
   4. He wanted to seek his fortune.
   5. Being so small, he was able to hurt the ogre from inside the ogre's stomach, causing the ogre to release the noble's daughter.
   6. The noble rewarded One-Inch Boy with half of his lands.
   7. He brought his parents to live in the palace in Kyoto.

Page 61

   A. 1. charm
      2. scabbard
      3. dense
      4. ancient
      5. ogre
      6. miniature
      7. journey
      8. persisted
      9. lacquer
   B. 1. unsheathed
      2. marveled
      3. fortune
      4. coincidence
      5. tremendous

Page 62

   1. Answers will vary. A possible answer is: In spite of his small size, One-Inch Boy was a good, helpful son.
   2. Answers will vary. A possible answer is: His parents loved him and wanted to help him achieve his dreams.
   3. Answers will vary. A possible answer is: The boatman was a kind and caring person.
   4. Answers will vary. A possible answer is: The people in the palace liked One-Inch Boy and enjoyed being with him.
   5. Answers will vary. A possible answer is: One-Inch Boy was very brave. Despite his size, he tried to defend the noble's daughter.
   6. Answers will vary. A possible answer is: The noble was grateful to One-Inch Boy. He was a very generous person.

Page 63

   Part 1: 3, 1, 4, 2, 5
   Part 2: 10, 9, 6, 7, 8
   Part 3: 13, 11, 12

Page 66

   1. He thought he was the wisest person in the land.
   2. They were afraid of him and thought he could use his magic to change them into something like a pig or a flowerpot.
   3. She said he couldn't change anything, even a caterpillar into a butterfly, and her cow was smarter.
   4. As the conversation was passed from one person to another, the facts were changed each time. Finally, it was said that the milkmaid had challenged the magician to a contest to see who was smarter. The winner would become governor.
   5. She was good-natured and she thought she should share her wisdom if people wanted her to do it.
   6. She said that the magician couldn't even remember to put on his shoes before he went outside.
   7. Answers will vary.

Page 67

   1. a. governor
      b. magician
      c. shoemaker
      d. blacksmith
      e. innkeepers
      f. milkmaid
      g. baker
      h. seamstress
      i. judges
      j. town crier
      k. teacher
      l. farmer
      m. carpenter
      n. laundress
   2. milkmaid, shoemaker, blacksmith, innkeepers
   3. solemn, elegant

Page 68

   Answers will vary. Possible answers include:
   Magician
   easily confused
   forgetful
   pompous
   boastful
   angry
   Milkmaid
   quick-thinking
   self-assured
   confident
   good-natured
   Both
   ambitious
   anxious to be governor

   Paragraphs should use the words and phrases listed in the Venn diagram.

Page 69

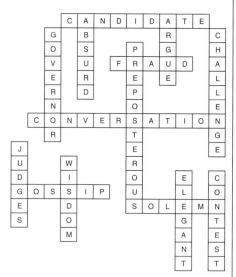

Page 72

1. Answers may vary. Possible answers are: He was jealous. He didn't like the way Jordan always made comments about why he didn't win.
2. He ran fast from the start and didn't have enough energy at the end to surge ahead. Jordan ran faster at the end of the race.
3. Grandpa Morgan was coming to see the race, and Zach had told his grandfather that he was the best runner on the team.
4. competing against yourself and trying to better your record each time you ran
5. No matter how good (fast) you are, there will always be someone better.
6. He realized that Zach was placing too much importance on trying to be the best runner; that Zach thought his grandfather wouldn't care as much about him if he wasn't a good runner. Grandpa wanted to let Zach know that running wasn't everything and that he loved Zach no matter what.

Page 73

1. a. competition
   b. competitor
   c. competitive
2. a. congratulations
   b. congratulate
3. a. challenging
   b. challenge
   c. challenger

4. a. event
   b. eventful

Page 74

A. 2, 4, 1, 5, 3, 6
B. 1. noun
   2. verb
   3. verb
   4. noun
   5. noun
   6. verb
C. Sentences will vary. "Record" must be used as a noun in one sentence and as a verb in the other sentence.

Page 75

Writings will vary, but must include the ideas stated in the prompt.

Page 78

1. warm weather, delicate yellow flowers
2. She wanted to give the boat to her brother for his birthday.
3. She tried to hold onto the tree, swim for shore, hold onto a rock, and then called for help.
4. She thought Amy had gone swimming and that was a foolish thing to do that time of year.
5. Answers will vary, but students are most likely to conclude that she was foolish to take the chance she did; if the neighbor had not appeared she might have drowned.
6. Answers will vary. Possible answer: If you spend too much time talking, it may be too late to solve the problem or help. It's better to help someone in danger first, and then explain why they shouldn't have placed themselves in danger.

Page 79

A. 1. version
   2. scolded
   3. I declare
   4. inched
   5. stuffed
   6. lecture
   7. current
   8. foolish
B. to stay afloat in an upright position by moving legs in a bicycling motion
C. to tell what you think about something in a scolding or an angry way

Page 80

Answers will vary.

Page 81

Alphabetical order: adjusted, Amy, balance, cloak, current, declare, delicate, drown, foolish, lecture, limb, neighbor, realized, scold, surprised, tread, version, wobbled

Page 84

1. a flying steed
   unicorn with diamond mane and sapphire horn
   painted creatures
   beasts with emerald hair
   dancing rabbits
   purple sheep
   birds with glowing, patchwork wings
   satin swans
2. New York, Zanzibar
3. imaginary kingdoms
4. Answers will vary, but should indicate yes because he/she is able to see many pictures in the shapes formed by the kaleidoscope.
5. Answers will vary.

Page 85

1. a. fantastic
   b. satin
   c. spiral
   d. verdant
   e. treasured
   f. mosaic
   g. patchwork
   h. geometric
   i. braided
   j. prancing
   k. crescent
   l. gallant
   m. bizarre
2. crystal, serpentine, jade, diamond, sapphire, ruby, golden, emerald, gems, jewels

Page 86
1. Any three of these:
   bet<u>ween</u>, tanger<u>ine</u>
   st<u>ar</u>, biz<u>arre</u>
   s<u>ea</u>, fr<u>ee</u>
   h<u>air</u>, everywh<u>ere</u>
   s<u>eems</u>, dr<u>eams</u>
   <u>on</u>, g<u>one</u>
2. evergr<u>een</u>, scr<u>een</u>
   f<u>ar</u>, Zanzib<u>ar</u>
   unic<u>orn</u>, h<u>orn</u>
   win<u>gs</u>, sprin<u>gs</u>
3. a. scene, serpentine, evergreen,
      screen, between, tangerine
   b. star, bizarre, far, Zanzibar

Page 87
1. <u>Real</u>
   golden summer sunsets
   brown oak and evergreen
   a deep-jade flowing river
   golden bridge
   <u>Imaginary</u>
   ruby sea
   beasts with emerald hair
   purple sheep
   a flock of birds with glowing,
   patchwork wings
2. Answers will vary.

Page 90
1. 1776
2. They have few supplies, they work
   very hard, they must make
   everything for themselves, and the
   journey is too difficult.
3. He is in charge when his father is
   away. He takes care of the fields
   and the cattle.
4. Answers will vary. Possible answer:
   His parents may not have been
   able to read and write.
5. Yes, de Anza was a good leader.
   He kept the caravan moving, he
   cared for the ill, and he gave cheer
   to the people.
6. organizing a large caravan at the
   beginning of the day, finding food
   and water for the animals, dust and
   alkali in the desert, bitter cold and
   snow, fording the river, loss of
   animals, no wood for fires
7. The letter has to go by sailing ship
   and mule train.

Page 91
A. 1. strayed
   2. fording
   3. caution
   4. caravan
   5. comforts
   6. progress
   7. alkali
   8. accompanied
   9. New Spain
   10. settlements
B. 1. survived
   2. galleon
   3. construction
   4. despondent
   5. bitterly
   6. celebrated
   7. exchanged
   8. challenge

Page 92
Verbs: Answers will vary.
Pronouns:
   1. galleon
   2. message
   3. native people
   4. animals
   5. My family and I
   6. soldiers
   7. Pima Indians
   8. Juan Bautista de Anza OR
      our leader

Page 93
Sequence of Events: 5, 3, 2, 4, 6, 1
Generalizing:
   1. Answers will vary. Possible answer:
      Few people made the journey by
      land from New Spain to Alta
      California because the weather and
      deserts made traveling difficult and
      the journey by ship was dangerous
      too.
   2. There was rich land, they could
      have farms and ranches, and they
      could be the first settlers of a new
      land.

Page 96
1. the individual medley at the county
   swim meet
2. Answers will vary, but may include
   words such as: anxious, prepared,
   in condition, ready, confident.
3. butterfly, backstroke, breastroke,
   freestyle
4. There were flags overhead near
   the end of the pool.
5. Opinions may vary as to whether

he actually won. "He was a winner"
might also mean that he did his
best, gave it his all, and/or had
prepared himself as thoroughly as
he could.
6. Answers will vary.

Page 97
A. 5, 6, 1, 4, 3, 2
B. 1. b
   2. a
   3. c
   4. a

Page 98
<u>swam</u>: undulated, flew down the lane,
broke the surface, stretched, slicing
into the water, reached, pulled,
glided, powered off the wall, slid
<u>walk</u>: Synonyms and sentences
will vary.

Page 99
<u>simile</u>: turning like the blades of a
windmill (Mark's arms, windmill)
<u>metaphor</u>: He was potential energy
personified (Mark, potential energy);
a speeding missile bound for the
finish (Mark, missile)
<u>personification</u>: The rough texture bit
into his fingertips. (wall is said to bite)

Page 102
1. Ella's property was rocky and hilly.
   Gretta's property had planted
   fields, orchards, and water.
2. She terraced and cultivated the
   hills. She took water from the river
   when it was needed.
3. Gretta thought that Ella used
   magic words.
4. Gretta thought she was growing
   more fruit because of the words
   she was using.
5. She tricked her into thinking taking
   care of the tree was magic. She
   brought her new fruit trees and
   planted them for her. She showed
   her what she had to do to be
   successful.
6. Ella meant that the fruit was
   wonderful, lovely, and delicious
   (enchanting) but not magic.

Page 103

Ella
satisfied
hard working
kind
helpful
cared for her crops
didn't complain
made the most of things
clever

Gretta
dishonest
didn't want to work for what she got
wanted to be important
envious
sneaky
thieving

Both
landowners
farmers

Page 104

A. 1. sturdy
   2. misfortune
   3. complain
   4. terracing
   5. cultivating
   6. prune
   7. worthless
   8. orchards
   9. prosperous
   10. inherited

B. 1. Any six of these: orchards, crops, fruit, weeds, carrots, blossom pears, vegetables, sprout, apple, tree, new growth
   2. Any six of these: planted, water, terracing, cultivating, gathered, prepare, trim, replant, prune
   3. property

Page 105

1. knot–not, sew–so, there–their, pair–pear, dew–do, knight–night, deer–dear, ewe–you, whole–hole, heir–air, knead–need, rein–rain
2. a. for, whole, four, hole
   b. pear, wait, weight, pair
   c. there, their, see, sea

Page 108

1. Their planet was taken over by worms that were eating everything.
2. All the other planets were too crowded.
3. dispose of them in a black hole
4. garden, air swim, work in the science lab, read, watch TV, look out the window, space walk

5. The narrator mentions having run out of books to read and not seeing a library in five years. The first thing the narrator asked upon landing on the new planet was directions to a library.
6. Answers will vary. Possible answer: In a park in a city on the planet earth
7. They saw the skeletons of creatures similar to themselves. They were being chased by creatures with nets.

Page 109

1. The Maiasaura looked like Aunt Worima; when they saw a picture of *Psittacosaurus* displays, the narrator said, "There are others here just like us." Dad said, "That's us."
2. Answers will vary, but three possibilities should be given.
3. Endings will vary, but must include the Worims being captured.

Page 110

1. noxious
2. plagued, communication, garbled
3. designed
4. heavily populated
5. mingle
6. anchored, transport
7. scenery
8. asteroid
9. intergalactic
10. etiquette
11. hitched
12. deserted
13. gigantic
14. disposing

Page 111

anchor	2	garbled	2
communication	5	gigantic	3
deserted	3	gravity	3
designed	2	intergalactic	5
etiquette	3	mingle	2
murals	2	satellite	3
museum	3	scenery	3
noxious	2	skeletons	3
plagued	1	transport	2
populated	4		

Page 114

1. liked talking to her, listening to her stories about the past and Mom; G-G-Ma listens, laughs at Sally's jokes, and gives hugs
2. a cake, dinner, a card, a poem
3. She had everything she needed—clothes, aprons, figurines, knick-knacks, towels
4. Because she didn't think she could take care of it, and maybe the kitten would find a home somewhere else.
5. She had a dog and her mother said one pet was enough.
6. She convinced her mother that G-G-Ma should have the kitten. Mother got the supplies needed and planned to take the kitten to the vet.

Page 115

1. a. doorknob
   b. everywhere
   c. leftover
   d. everything
   e. knickknacks
   f. anything
   g. great-grandmother
   h. ninety-one
   i. outside
   j. sometime
   k. birthday
2. a. too
   b. to
   c. to
   d. too
   e. to

Page 116

A. 1. She is
   2. did not
   3. I will
   4. can not
   5. she will

6. I would
7. we will
8. you will
9. I have
B. 1. It's
2. its
3. It's
4. it's
5. Its
C. Answers will vary.

Page 117

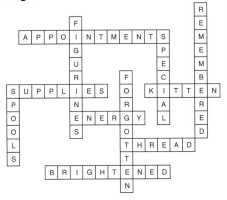

Page 120

1. He had passed these rules: that all the gold should belong to the greatest king in the universe, and that he was the greatest king in the universe.
2. He thought the moon was filled with gold. When the phases of the moon made the moon seem to shrink and grow, he thought someone was stealing his gold. He believed the plan to build a tower to the moon would allow him to reach the gold.
3. The advisor had run out of people to accept the role of second-wisest person, and the goatherd agreed to help the king.
4. If the goatherd did not find a way for the king to reach the moon, the king would imprison both the goatherd and the advisor.
5. He dreamed about standing on something to reach an apple in the tree.
6. Answers will vary. Some students may say the goatherd was clever because he knew all about goats and making cheese, and he knew that it was a mistake to take something from the bottom of the tower. Others may think him stupid because he suggested that a tower could be built to reach the moon.
7. Sentences will vary, but should include the idea that the tower

collapsed, taking the foolish king with it.

Page 121

A. 1. provide
2. impossible
3. universe
4. carpenter
5. command
6. proclaimed
7. entitled
8. treasury
9. telescope
10. crescent
11. royal
12. beyond
B. highness, majesty

Page 122

Royal Advisor
Problems:
had to find the second-wisest person
might get thrown into jail too

Solutions:
came across two goatherds
helped the goatherd

Goatherd
Problems:
had to come up with a plan

Solutions:
dreamed about picking fruit

King Alexander
Problems:
thought gold was being stolen
needed help to reach the moon
still couldn't reach the moon

Solutions:
decided to catch the thief
sent his advisor to find the second-wisest person
demanded that something be taken from the bottom

Page 123

Retellings will vary.

Page 126

1. It was a family tradition to sew items and enter them in the sewing competition at the fair. The ring was a family tradition, given from one family member to another for over 100 years.
2. Answers will vary. Some students may feel Anna's parents were wrong to think she had lost the ring when she insisted that she did not

take it and spent so much time looking for it. Others may feel that the parents had a right to think Anna had lost the ring because that seemed to be the only reasonable explanation.
3. She spent so much time looking for it; she tried very hard to find the ring.
4. She saw a crow fly into the bedroom and take a silver bead from the sewing basket.
5. In sentence two of the story: sunlight streamed through the **open** window.
6. Anna climbed a ladder to get to the crow's nest high up in a pine tree. She rummaged around in the nest and found the ring among a number of other shiny objects. Climbing was frightening; she was very careful and didn't look down.
7. to wear for good luck until the soccer game; to show that she trusted Anna with the ring

Page 127

A. 1. tradition
2. embroidering
3. admiring
4. extension
5. ridiculous
6. fretted
7. suspiciously
8. serious
B. admire–ing
embroider–ing
fret–ed
suspicious (suspect)–ly
extend–sion

Page 128

Sequence: 8, 7, 4, 1, 3, 5, 6, 2

Page 129

Answers will vary.

Page 132

1. He earned the money weeding and hoeing during spring vacation and bought it from Manuel when the Martinez family moved.
2. The bicycle represented independence—being able to stay after school to play baseball because he didn't have to take the bus home.
3. His parents were farm workers and had to go where there were crops being planted or harvested.
4. Eduardo was angry and upset because his parents were loading the van in preparation for another move.
5. He helped his younger brothers with their homework; he got them ready for bed and off to school; he was concerned that the schoolbooks needed to be returned before the family left; he wanted to explain to his teacher and classmates why he was leaving.
6. He thought about being able to buy a baseball bat and playing ball with his brothers when they were older. He dreamed of playing in the big leagues someday.

Bonus: The title is what the umpire shouts when a baseball game is ready to begin. The exclamation mark signifies something said with emphasis.

Page 133

1. a. bicicleta
   b. hijo
2. a. gravel
   b. neighbors
   c. science
   d. collected
   e. homework
   f. travel
   g. promised
   h. practice
   i. foreman
   j. maybe
3. Sentences will vary.

Page 134

A. 1. anymore, anywhere
   2. everyone, everything, everybody
   3. anywhere, somewhere
   4. somewhere, somehow
   5. outside
   6. overnight
   7. baseball
   8. notebook
   9. homework
   10. backpack
   11. outfield

B. Sentences will vary.

Page 135

Answers will vary. Possible answers are listed below.

Eduardo

helpful
helped his brothers with homework

hardworking/independent
earned his own money
worked during vacations

dependable
wanted books returned to school
helped his parents

studious
liked science
was catching up with his schoolwork
liked school

athletic
played on the baseball team
rode a bike

insecure
didn't like moving and new schools

hopeful
thought about being a baseball player

kind
complimented Roberto